REINVENTING SENIOR LIVING
The Art of Living with
Purpose, Passion & Joy

Published by Impact Publishing™, Orlando, FL.

Impact Publishing™ is a registered trademark.

Printed in the United States of America.

ISBN: 978-0-9983690-9-9
LCCN: 2017947014

This publication is designed to provide accurate and authoritative information with regard to the subject matter covered. It is sold with the understanding that the publisher is not engaged in rendering legal, accounting, or other professional advice. If legal advice or other expert assistance is required, the services of a competent professional should be sought. The opinions expressed by the author in this book are not endorsed by Impact Publishing™ and are the sole responsibility of the author rendering the opinion.

Most Impact Publishing™ titles are available at special quantity discounts for bulk purchases for sales promotions, premiums, fundraising, and educational use. Special versions or book excerpts can also be created to fit specific needs.

For more information, please write:
Impact Publishing™
520 N. Orlando Ave, #2
Winter Park, FL 32789
or call 1.877.261.4930

REINVENTING SENIOR LIVING
The Art of Living with
Purpose, Passion & Joy

By **LAURENCE J. PINO, ESQ.**

Impact Publishing™
Winter Park, Florida

CONTENTS

This book is dedicated to my mother, Maria Giordano Pino, who inspired the very purpose, passion, and joy behind the book and, even more importantly, Tuscan Gardens itself.

PREFACE

Before I launch into this book, I thought it would only be appropriate to sketch out a very brief history of how the concept of the book came about and, with that, the tremendous debt of gratitude I owe to so many individuals who have made this book a possibility.

As I explain in some detail in the upcoming "Introduction," the concept of Tuscan Gardens emerged in 2010, but we did not actually get started until 2014 when my partners and I bought a parcel of property in Venice, Florida. One of my partners, Chris Young, told me that it was critical for me to put in writing what I had been talking about for the prior several years. We were about to do a "design charrette" (a term I had never heard of) where we were going to be sitting down with the architect, interior designer, engineers, functional consultants and specialists, landscapers, and so forth. Chris was concerned that I make as clear as possible what it was I wanted Tuscan Gardens to look like.

I told him I would and went about writing the first of what I called an "Enterprise Charter." The Enterprise Charter started off at something like six pages, but by the time I finished, it was close to thirty pages. The Enterprise Charter formed the foundation for the development of our first community in Venice which I expanded for Palm Coast, Delray Beach, and others.

Along the way, however, I felt that while the Enterprise Charter was good in certain ways, it lacked the depth to convey my thoughts to the many stakeholders who were involved in the operation of Tuscan Gardens and in the senior living industry as a whole. So, I felt I needed to expand the scope of the Charter into something I could use to convey my thoughts at an even broader level.

Spurred on by Chris and my long-suffering partners Buddy Smith, Sean Casterline, Bill Johnston, and my wife, Janet, I decided to convert the Charter into a published book. My thanks go out to each one of them for their faith and trust, as well as the support and wisdom they have continued to show day by day as we jointly expand the footprint of Tuscan Gardens and, through it, our involvement in senior living.

Along with my partners, a vote of encouragement also came from my three-decade friend and former legal partner, Jack W. Dicks, Esq., who, in conjunction with his partner, Nick D. Nanton, and daughter, Lindsay Dicks, operate several publishing companies, one of which is the publisher of this book. His words were loud and clear: Write the book and I'll get it published and out to the community faster than any other publisher can. Thank you, Jack, for all your advice and counsel.

My first call, after I decided to pursue the book project, was to a colleague with whom I have worked for close to two decades – Amy Detwiler. She has been a researcher for me in my prior lifetime, an instructional writer for the many manuals my companies have produced over the years, a writer par excellence at every level, an editor, kindred spirit, and friend. I asked her if she was willing to assist me to expand our footprint, not only with Tuscan Gardens, but also in what others were doing in the senior living space.

It took Amy approximately ten seconds of holding back her excitement before blurting out her unrestricted and unbridled enthusiasm. A year later, here we are. It goes without saying that had Amy not said "yes" that day, this book would not be here this day.

And finally, I want to thank so many individuals for what they have taught me from the ground up in the industry. Architects Kevin Bessolo, Tim Baker and Stephen Park are true experts in the craft, not only in design and architecture, but also in creating senior living spaces which resonate. Lisa Cini of Mosaic Design has operated as our interior designer and as a functional expert in every aspect of senior living environments. Suzanne Alford from Life Care Services (LCS), with years of experience in senior living, remained our go-to person, particularly in Memory Care. She had answers when we didn't even know what the questions were. And speaking of LCS – Life Care Services of Des Moines, Iowa – the journey with them has been nothing less than enlightening. As a respected third-party operator in the senior living industry covering the full continuum of care, LCS has huge resources at its disposal. By collaborating with LCS, I have learned not only delivery models which work, as well as those that don't, and refinements to what can make the resident experience more meaningful.

John Wiseman from CORE Construction has been a miraculous supporter of the Tuscan dream in bringing all of the resources of CORE Construction to the table as our contractor. And Bill Sims and Rob Gall from HJ Sims, along with their committed attorney, David Williams of Atlanta, have fought hard to make sure that our first few communities had the financial backing they needed to go from concept to reality.

I could go on, of course, but the list of individuals with whom I have worked just keeps growing as this Preface may very well if I try to name them all. In short, my appreciation goes out to all of them in what is no doubt turning out to be a collaborative pursuit and a lifelong passion for all of us.

INTRODUCTION

We're Italian, and as Italians, the concept of putting our parents in any type of "facility" was culturally taboo. In any conversation I ever had with Mom and Dad, it was always out of the question. Only two options ever existed:

1. Have them live with one of the children (my sister or myself); or in the event that number one was an impossibility –

2. Have our parents cared for in their own home by a dedicated caregiver.

As it turns out, we never faced that question with my father. Dad passed away six months after he and my mother celebrated their 50th anniversary, at the all-too-young age of 72 in 1995. It was quick and devastating. As a result, we moved Mom out of the home they shared and into her own home seven minutes away from my family's home.

Mom lived there, abiding the circumstances and on her own, until she contracted pneumonia in 2002 and was hospitalized for almost six months and intubated for close to three. Over the next six months, she went from Florida Hospital to a rehab facility, back to her home, back to Florida Hospital, to another rehab facility, and to her home. She did that on four different occasions in a round-robin fashion until we decided to bring her home for good and hire a fulltime, live-in 24/7 caregiver.

During the next 12 years, she was admitted to hospice twice – and kicked out twice – after hospice was economically exasperated by her longevity. It might have been a surprise to them, but not to us. It's what we call the "Tuscan Way!"

Mom eventually passed away in January of 2014, just shy of her 92nd birthday. Over that time, she had just three sets of caregivers who did an extraordinary job taking care of her.

As much as private in-home caregiving had advantages, disadvantages surfaced. First, of course, was the substantial economic cost; second was the lack of social interaction and programming. At a certain point, my mother and a caregiver, regardless of their sense of closeness, simply had very little left to talk about and very little left to share.

So, from time to time – and the "Italian Contract" notwithstanding – I would check out the market to see if a better alternative developed. Every time I did, I was disappointed and kept Mom at home.

In 2010, for personal as well as economic reasons, I went to the market yet again to see if there were opportunities for me to put Mom someplace with which I felt comfortable, if not enthusiastic. Again, I just couldn't find any place I was prepared to accept and certainly not close by.

Because of that, in trying to figure out how to balance the economic cost of keeping Mom at home and the personal values which come from putting her someplace worthy of her, it occurred to me that I had been unable to find a place in which I would be prepared to put my own mother. The question that kept surfacing was, "Why?"

Eventually, I asked myself the fundamental question: "What would it have to look like for me to be willing to put my own mother in it?" In other words, in what sort of community could I place my mother happily, unreservedly and with the full expectation that her life would be enriched, not diminished, by making the transition?

That was the seminal moment – in mid-2010 – that ultimately resulted in the conceptualization of Tuscan Gardens. In the intervening years, I have continued to refine the concept, which at its heart crystallizes the experience I wanted to create for my own mother and offer it to the general public.

It began strangely enough, not with a view of tangible components – drapes, walls or flooring – but rather with values and feelings. Defining the atmosphere through those value statements allowed me to conceptualize an environment where the values might bud and blossom.

It had to be about:

- **Compassion and Empathy**

- **Grace, Intimacy, and Vitality**

- **Laughter, Family, and a Sense of Humor**

- **Casual Elegance**

- **Vibrant Energy and Lightness**

- **Extraordinary Service**

During the past seven years, I have immersed myself in the senior living industry to learn from the ground up the best way to bring this "values vision" to life. While my mother was the motivation, my own passion for the pursuit soon became the key driver.

What I've come to discover is that the rapidly changing senior living marketplace is becoming increasingly competitive and challenging. It has been moving from a commodity-based enterprise to an experience-based one. New players, like myself, are creating a highly-differentiated value proposition that pinpoints and delivers the experiences seniors want today and anticipates those that will be desired in the future, particularly in terms of the high-energy Baby Boomer as a target resident population. Reinventing senior living for these 70 million sophisticated and cultured individuals who embrace a much more active lifestyle than their parents or grandparents embraced will require a compelling and provocative resident experience that appeals to them right out of the gate.

Along the way, I've had the ability to learn from those who have been involved in the senior living industry for 20 to 30 years. At the same time, nothing up to that point had "felt" quite right for my own mother. So, while the industry might benefit from someone willing to ask "why," the good news is that there are any number of us attempting to solve for the answer.

Since those earlier days, Tuscan Gardens has launched multiple communities from full operations to early development stages. And others in the space have continued to push the edge.

Gratifyingly, the industry has been welcoming to people

like me and others who have stretched and reframed the product in a radically different way. There's been a recognition and an acknowledgment that we aren't limited by what and how things used to be done.

Tuscan Gardens, like other new entrants in the industry, seeks to successfully reinvent the senior living product in terms of both infrastructure and programming. We place the resident at the center of the process. We imagine the person and the lifestyle and then design the living space to support that rather than design the living space and seek to shoehorn the resident into what we've predetermined for them.

In observance of our tagline, *The Art of Living*, Tuscan Gardens dares to ask, "What is living as a senior and what does that mean?"

Tuscan Gardens provides the landscape for seniors to enjoy the fruits harvested from a life well lived. It was created as a continuum of care where seniors can live and thrive with purpose, passion, and joy, in whatever stage of life they find themselves – independent living, assisted living or memory care. The result is an invigorating life of new ideas and experiences with the wisdom, time, and curiosity to enjoy them all.

Throughout this book, you will be presented with a landscape of the senior living industry – its current status and what it has the potential to be. You will be challenged to formulate your own definition of senior living – from infrastructure to cuisine to programming – and I will illustrate my conceptualization of that experience, using Tuscan Gardens as an example.

Without espousing or sanctioning any one particular brand name, you will be introduced to various companies working in the senior living space and their products that are doing their own part to reinvent the senior living experience.

I'll examine the operational environment that sets the stage for a rewarding experience, not only for the residents, but also for the staff charged with crafting a homelike environment filled with care, consideration, and love.

And, most importantly of all, I will maintain an open conversation, as well as an invitation to all those very talented senior living ThoughtLeaders® who have joined the fray for their own reasons and seek to expand the space for the benefit of us all.

CHAPTER 1

TUSCANY
WHERE IT ALL BEGAN

*The Tuscans have the faculty of making much of common things
and converting small occasions into great pleasures.*
~ Henry James

For the Pino family – my parents, myself, my wife and my children — *The Art of Living* is heavily influenced by an Italian lifestyle or, more to the point, Tuscan living. It's been part of our DNA for nearly 230 years when my mother's family, the Giordanos, founded and established their businesses "under the Tuscan sun" – not really, by the way, it was actually in the rich southern landscape of Puglia.

An aristocratic family of noble origin, the Giordanos descended from Dukes within Italian royalty, originally from Rome. The story that has been passed down is that the family went into exile in the 15th Century for unknown reasons (I could only begin to conjecture), making their home among the high-born aristocracy in the southern part of Italy.

Eventually, the Giordanos settled in Naples in the late 1700s, starting their company – G.A. Giordano & Company, in 1788. By the mid-1800s, my mother's grandfather, Giuseppe Giordano, relocated the family from Naples to Bari, the capital of the county Puglia, a prosperous port city on the shores of the Adriatic Sea very near the "heel" of Italy's boot.

Giuseppe invested in the fur business that established the Giordanos as prominent merchants throughout southern Italy. Even with the mild climate, the furs sold well, first in Italy, then throughout all of Europe and eventually internationally, growing the business into a solid global enterprise.

A century and a half later, G.A. Giordano's great great grandson, Giuseppe married 15-year-old Leonarda, the 22nd child in her family. Together they had 17 children. While 17 came into the world, only 10 survived childhood – six sons and four daughters. Many died during outbreaks of influenza and cholera that swept through the southern part of Italy and ravaged families. Five of the sons were actively involved in the family fur business, including my mother's father, Armando.

Armando married Maria Nicoletta Accettura, one of just two pampered daughters of an equally wealthy and noble Southern Italian family. Maria's father, Vito Accettura, was mayor of their town, Ceglie Carbonata, located next to Bari.

The Giordanos were very well known throughout Bari and the surrounding counties. The sons worked together, each with a different responsibility within the fur business. Armando's role included sorting and grading the various furs. The wives remained within the family home, managing the households and the children. And, what a household it was.

My mother's childhood home, Il Palazzo Giordano, covered a whole city block in Bari. With 16 bedrooms, Il Palazzo Giordano was more a compound, than a single family home. It was there that my mother and her extended family lived, worked, and played. Each of my grandfather's brothers and sisters had a home within the massive compound for themselves, their spouses and children. These beautiful, spacious residences – separate, yet interconnected – housed my mother's aunts, uncles and some 30 cousins. I saw it for the first time at age 11 and now, more than 55 years later, the recollection still stirs me.

Sheltered within the walls of the compound was a huge central garden, as big as a city park, with manicured lawns, trees, and a grotto – completely isolated from the outside world. The garden contained a veritable jungle of fruit trees – fig, orange, tangerine, pomegranate, kumquat and persimmon – as well as palm trees, mimosas, rose bushes and an enormous selection of flowers. The gardener tended vegetables in one area. In another section was a wide, open field, large enough for cricket and other ball games that the cousins would invent. However, the children's favorite place of all was the grotto, a small rock cave that they spent hours in, home to all of their fantasies.

The furnishings and fixtures contained within the walls of the palazzo included heirloom items passed down from within the family and museum-quality art and sculpture. Oriental rugs covered black and white marble floors. Directly above this checkerboard sea, hand painted frescoes graced the ceilings.

Tiffany glass windows faced the street, each hand etched with the Giordano family coat of arms. The image in the crest displayed a central olive tree flanked by two rampant lions, rearing up on their hind legs, one forepaw raised above the other. Luscious, heavy velvet drapes blocked the fiery Italian sun in the summer and kept the large rooms cozy in the winter.

The palazzo contained room upon room of enormous mirrors, beautiful chests, elaborate tables, and luxuriously upholstered chairs and sofas, the wood ornately carved and gilded. Expensive artwork crowned each doorway, including old paintings, portraits, and detailed tapestries in muted colors.

The entire Giordano clan was expected to behave with the "galatea" – the strict observance of the manners, culture, and education of the aristocracy. That could not be compromised. The tradition of social class had to be maintained at all times. Every meal was a large scale production filled with beautiful china, crystal, linen, silver, and finely-crafted food served in an atmosphere of elegance and sophistication.

When the air grew cooler and the smell of autumn blew through the compound, the Giordanos moved to their family farm, la Masseria, for the harvest. For generations, my grandmother's family owned the beautiful farm, la Masseria, in the countryside outside of Bari. Scattered over the ancient farmland were acres and acres of almond trees, olive trees and grapevines.

Into this lap of luxury was born Maria Rosaria Pompei Anna Antonia Giordano – my mother. The year was 1922, the same one that saw Benito Mussolini rise to power as Prime Minister of Italy. From birth, Mom was surrounded by servants, chauffeurs, maids, and governesses.

My mother was the third of five children. The firstborn child of Armando and Maria Nicoletta was a son, Giuseppe – lovingly called Peppino – named after his paternal grandfather. The second, Leonarda or Leda for short, was named after her paternal grandmother. One boy, Vito, died in infancy. The last

Giordano child was my Uncle Mario, an irrepressible entrepreneur who actively joined the fur business at age 19. Mario worked in Italy, then Paraguay, finally settling in Argentina to raise and sell chinchilla pelts. If anyone sparked the entrepreneurial spirit in me, it was surely Zio Mario.

As youngsters, the Giordano children studied under the original Montessori nuns. Upon reaching age nine, they all attended boarding school in Rome – the boys at Mondragone, the girls at Collegio delle Dame Inglesi di Roma, the English school of the Catholic nuns in Rome. The collegio sat adjacent to Villa Torlonia, Mussolini's country home, and across the street from the Catacombs of St. Agnes: a more spectacular site would be hard to find.

For a little over 20 years, my mother lived this lifestyle of elegance, grace, and sophistication – that is, until World War II directly impacted both Bari and the Giordanos. As the Allies leapfrogged from Africa to Sicily into mainland Italy, heading east and north, the decision was made to locate the Allied Forces Regional Headquarters in Bari. No property better suited their needs than Il Palazzo Giordano. When the word came to leave and evacuate in October 1943, the Giordanos had only four hours to gather their belongings and retreat to la Masseria to live out the balance of the war.

Happily, la Masseria provided a comfortable life for the family and they had the opportunity to return to Il Palazzo for belongings and provisions as needed. During one such visit, Maria Rosaria Pompei Anna Antonia Giordano caught the eye of a rather bold, but friendly, young American soldier, Saverio (Sam) Pino.

Sam's background couldn't be more different than Maria's. The Pino family housed tomato farmers, hailing from a small village in Sicily called Saponara. His father, Sebastanio (Benjamin), immigrated to America at age 13, entering the country through the much-fabled Ellis Island Inspection Station. Benjamin settled in Philadelphia, started working immediately and sent money back home. One by one Benjamin brought his brothers and sisters over from the old country.

Of the 700 people in Saponara when I returned to visit in 1992, 85 were Pinos, and every single one embraced me as if I were a long-lost brother, beloved son or cherished cousin.

I share the story of my parents not only because I find it touching and uplifting, but also as a means of sharing my vision for Tuscan Gardens.

In the "Introduction," I made mention of seeking someplace worthy of Mom, perhaps understanding her history and background you can appreciate how difficult that proposition would be. Yet, her lifestyle wasn't simply elegant surroundings; it was also gracious living. Frankly, when my mother married my father, she left behind that luxury and lived a much more modest lifestyle, but one that was no less gracious. She never lost that sense of being a member of the nobility – whether in Il Palazzo Giordano or an apartment in South Jersey. In being her child, and being raised by her, it afforded me the opportunity to form attributes of character and attributes of taste. From my father, I gained an appreciation for heritage, tradition, and honesty. From both, I learned what it meant to feel like family from the moment you walk in the door.

So, these two wonderful people – their histories, their backgrounds, and their character – have informed the Tuscan Gardens approach. Not only have I attempted to recreate the gracious life my mother lived, but also the warmth and intimacy of my father's loving Sicilian family. It's not just about elegance, but about being embraced.

As you read on, remember the histories of both my mother and my father and consider how the atmosphere and values of both have been embedded within Tuscan Gardens and how they can be leveraged for any senior living community seeking an elevated experience for its residents.

One final note of interest: Beautiful Palazzo Giordano, when it finally passed out of the family's hands, was converted into a 16-bedroom senior living facility. Rather poetic, wouldn't you say?

CHAPTER 2

THE CURRENT STATE OF SENIOR LIVING

Grow old along with me. The best is yet to be.
~ Robert Browning

In the previous chapter, you got a taste of what *The Art of Living* means to the Giordanos and the Pinos. For others, it may be dictated by different culture, heritage or bond. It's the stage upon which someone wishes to age with the accompanying décor, foods, lifestyle, and programming that give their life meaning. So, while throughout this book you'll see *The Art of Living* described in the ways that it's been brought to life at Tuscan Gardens, realize that living well at its essence is created in whatever context the individual desires it to happen.

NICHE COMMUNITIES

Certainly, several senior living communities exist which cater to a faith-based demographic (without excluding individuals from other theological viewpoints). Others cater to armed services veterans and their spouses, individuals retired from certain lines of work, and people of specific ethnicities. These niche or affinity communities represent a growing trend in senior living. Current statistics report approximately 100 of these communities currently exist, representing shared interests, sexuality, education, religions, professional backgrounds, hobbies or lifestyles. Congregating with people who share similar backgrounds on views on life could define *The Art of Living* for themselves for many seniors.

Perhaps the most intriguing of these niche communities is the university-based retirement communities (UBRCs) located on or near college campuses. Andrew Carle, founder of George Mason University's program in senior housing administration coined the term "university-based retirement community" in 2006. It's estimated that 100 UBRCs currently exist, but expect that number to grow as Baby Boomers seek to maintain their vibrant lifestyles.

Some noteworthy UBRCs include:

- Kendal at Hanover, connected with Dartmouth College in Hanover, NH, offers four senior living options (Independent Living to Memory Care) and full-length to mini courses at the college's Institute for Lifelong Education at Dartmouth (ILEAD). Dartmouth-Hitchcock Medical Center also hosts an onsite clinic for residents. Other Kendal UBRCs include Kendal at Ithaca, near Cornell University, Kendal on Hudson, Kendal at Oberlin, Kendal at Granville, Kendal at Home, Kendal-Crosslands Communities and Kendal at Lexington.

- Marylhurst University in Lake Oswego, OR works with UBRC Mary's Woods at Marylhurst. Wi-Fi, free computer classes, a complimentary tablet on move-in, and deep discounts on classes are a few of the great amenities provided.

- Residents at Holy Cross Village at Notre Dame (my alma mater) are just 1,000 feet from Holy Cross College. Residents can consider the campus an adjunct to their own community with free use of the college library and fitness center. Access to athletic events and the ability to audit classes at Holy Cross and St. Mary's College round out the offerings.

- Lasell Village, at Lasell College in Newton, MA, requires residents to complete 450 hours of learning or fitness activities annually. Residents have their own academic dean and each building at the community has a classroom, studio, library or fitness facility.

- Oak Hammock, at the University of Florida in Gainesville,

offers classes through its Institute for Learning in Retirement not only to residents, but also Gainesville citizens age 55 and older. Classes are taught by current or retired faculty from the university or other institutions.

While the foregoing are noteworthy examples, other UBRC communities include Barclay Friends and Chandler Hall in Pennsylvania; University Retirement Community and Vi at Palo Alto in California; The Admiral at the Lake in Illinois; Green Hills Retirement Community in Iowa; Meadowood Retirement Community in Indiana; The Lathrop Communities in Massachusetts and Collington in Maryland.

Successful UBRCs are as unique as the residents they house. However, some attributes can be considered common to UBRCs:

- **Close proximity to campus**

- **Formalized programming between the university and the UBRC that encourages intergenerational diversity and a range of activity**

- **Full senior housing services (The continuum of care from Independent Living to Assisted Living)**

- **Strong alumni base (generally at least 10% of the community population are alumni, former faculty or former university employees)**

- **Sound financial planning with a documented financial relationship between the university and UBRC**

Considering mental stimulation and lifelong learning are critical components of a vibrant senior lifestyle, providing this type of access to intellectual and cultural opportunities is sure to continue to show strong growth. Even those communities not situated on-campus can provide in-community or web-based learning sessions, which will help them attract and maintain educationally-minded residents.

Of course, the commonality in an ideal senior living community could be nothing more than liking the same music. Parrotheads of the world will unite at Latitude Margaritaville, a 55-plus active adult mixed-use community set to break ground in Daytona Beach, Florida.

The joint venture between Minto Group, an Ottawa, Canada-based real estate development and property management company, and Margaritaville Holdings is reported to be "golf-cart" friendly and include a fitness center, retail area, bandshell, and beachfront club. Move-ins are expected to begin in the third quarter of 2018.

Aging in niche communities that represent or celebrate an intrinsic part of an individual's history or personality provides a sense of depth, recognition, and comfort – a richness that comes from sharing life's joys and sorrows with other like-minded people.

GENERATIONAL COHORTS

And, speaking of which, who are those like-minded people with whom today's senior may surround himself?

Birth Years	Generation
1901-1924	G.I. or Greatest Generation
1925-1942	Silent Generation
1943-1964	Baby Boomers
1965-1979	Generation X
1980-2000	Millennials
2001-2013	iGen or Generation Z

The generational cohorts listed above span roughly 20 years. While some Greatest Generation seniors survive, the groups largely influencing today's senior living industry are the Silent Generation and, by sheer numbers, Baby Boomers. Due to being born and coming of age at roughly the same point in history, these individuals share similar experiences and often display similar attitudes. Greater insight into these experiences and attitudes can be gleaned by researching the time in history when the generation tended to dominate society, typically during their middle age years of 40 to 60.

Much has been said about the Baby Boomers and their impact on the senior living industry. Considering that the 65+ population will grow at an annual rate of 2.93% at least over the next five years, demand for senior housing should remain strong for many years to come.

That being said, however, the Baby Boomers will have less of an impact in the short term. Considering that the average age of entry into senior housing is 80+ years, look for the Baby Boomers to really begin stretching senior housing resources in the year 2023 and beyond. Even now, the annual growth in the 80 and over population is reported to be 1.7%, according to the U.S. Census, which bests overall population growth by a whopping 0.9%.

Now is the time to prepare for the largest influx of Baby Boomers in the early 2020s by either designing or retrofitting senior properties, primarily in terms of amenities. Additionally, it might be wise to take into account Generation Xers who make up the adult children of this target market, making a significant contribution to the decision-making process.

Adult children tend to strongly impact the senior housing decision. My entry into the senior housing industry attests to the veracity of this claim. Adult children are frequently highly involved in community selection. Statistically, half or more of a community's residents relocate from outside the market area to be nearer family. It makes sense that they would depend heavily on the opinions of these family members who are familiar with the geographic attributes of a given area.

Households headed by adult children (those aged 45 to 64 who are mostly likely to have a parent in the 80+ age range) tend to be declining in 34 states. As a group, these individuals tend to be mobile and move primarily for employment reasons. In Image 1 at the top of the following page, states represented in the lightest shades show growth of up to 4.9% and those in darkest shades (Texas, Utah, and Montana) 10% to 14.9%.

Image 1

Aging in place is contributing to growth in senior households aged 75 and above. As you might imagine with the graying of America, every state will feel the impact of these older households during the next five years as depicted by Image 2 below. The only wild card will be the degree of impact from a low of just over 3% in Rhode Island to 28% in Alaska. The top five states are Texas, Georgia, Colorado, Nevada, and Alaska. *(Shown as the darkest shades on Image 2)*

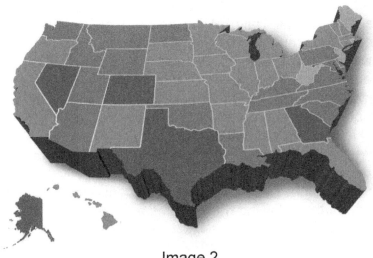

Image 2

As a member of the Baby Boom generation myself, Tuscan Gardens reflects not only the Tuscan lifestyle of my heritage, but the infrastructure, atmosphere, and programming that resonate with me generationally.

TYPES OF SENIOR LIVING OPTIONS

The plethora of senior living opportunities range from living at home (a.k.a. Aging in Place) to communities of varying sizes, amenities, and lifestyles.

Aging in Place refers to seniors remaining in their home safely, independently, and comfortably. Statistically, aging in place is the most preferred option among seniors with approximately 90 percent of adults over 65 reporting a desire to stay in their current residence.

In order to successfully age in place, seniors may require home modifications. Common home modifications include:

- **General:** Stair/hallway railings, non-skid flooring, ramps, stair lifts

- **Bathroom:** Shower/tub grab bars, walk-in shower/tub, handheld shower heads

- **Kitchen:** Sliding shelves

Of course, one of the primary benefits of well-designed community-based senior housing, like the options described below, is that these modifications are already in place and seniors need not invest the funds and time or undergo the stress in accomplishing these upgrades. But before we discuss those options, let's examine one more "aging in place" opportunity.

GRANNY PODS

According to The Center on Aging & Working at Boston College, one in five Americans live in households with two or more adult generations. "Temporary family health care dwellings" (aka granny pods or drop homes) have become a popular alternative for housing older family members on the same property as their adult children or grandchildren. It's a type of "age in place" configuration that allows families to live together, while offering some type of independence for all parties. However, these small, accessory dwellings require proper zoning, something many municipalities are refusing to grant.

Most recently, the state of Minnesota has permitted granny pods under certain requirements, except in cities that have chosen to prohibit them. Current "granny pod laws" include the following:

- Homes cannot exceed 300 square feet.

- Homes must be located on the property where the caregiver or relative lives.

- A medical professional must attest that the person occupying the home needs help with two or more daily activities.

Those coming down on the "anti-granny pod" side are St. Cloud, Minneapolis, St. Paul and a number of metro-area suburbs that have banned them or are likely to do so. Many municipalities cite the numerous "unknowns" surrounding these unique dwellings as the main reason for opting out. Several communities say they would like more time to study this new type of housing and how to deal with it before lifting restrictions.

Yet, unknowns won't satisfy the critical need for senior housing options. The demand for affordable senior housing in Minnesota is expected to increase by more than 50% over the next five years, according to a 2014 study by the Minnesota Housing Partnership.

Several granny pod builders, including NextDoor Housing, MedCottage, FabCab and the Home Store, are confident that opportunities exist, particularly in rural areas, despite restrictions in certain urban and suburban localities.

NextDoor Housing

NextDoor Housing has pioneered the granny pod concept in its native Minnesota. These "drop homes" offer a secure, functional environment designed by certified aging in place specialists. Each universally designed DropHome™ features fully accessible facilities to ensure safety and comfort. The frame itself drops to the ground so with one easy step seniors are right at home.

The DropHome™ is 30 feet long and 8 feet wide. It needs space to be installed and removed, for this process a standard 1-ton pickup truck is used. Homeowners should have a flat footprint of those dimensions and space to bring it in. People interested in this type of granny pod should check their local ordinances on square footage requirements for water run-off, which typically only applies to small lots.

A DropHome™ needs access to water and power, just like any other house. Ingeniously, it's completely designed to run off an existing residence. Thirty to fifty amp electrical service is recommended, and an insulated garden hose to a water source keep the pod running, no matter the weather.

NextDoor Housing's granny pods are designed to withstand severe weather and meet or exceed the construction standards for recreational vehicles. NextDoor Housing partnered with Homark Homes to build the pods and mount them on steel trailers.

MedCottage

An affordable alternative to nursing homes, MEDCottage is a mobile, modular medical dwelling designed to be temporarily placed on a caregiver's property for rehabilitation and extended care. Simply stated, it's a state-of-the-art hospital room with remote monitoring available so caregivers and family members have peace of mind knowing they are providing the best possible care.

Fundamental to family caregiving is proximity to the one needing care. There is a connection between the number of visits and the physical distance from family. Additionally, is the satisfaction factor, the experience must be enjoyable for both. People typically don't continue something that's not enjoyable or difficult to achieve. Closeness with a degree of privacy is huge in making this happen.

MEDCottages give families choices and real solutions when participating in extended care of loved ones. The MEDCottages models provide real solutions that encourage families to participate in caregiving while preserving one's privacy. MEDCottage is a division of N2Care, LLC. N2Care's products give families the ability to directly participate in their loved ones' recovery or extended care.

MEDCottage offers three distinct models:

- Garage Pod is designed for inside the garage. It comes in a kit so the homeowner can assemble inside a two-bay garage. The windows are HD monitors, framed as windows with a corresponding HD camera outside creating the illusion of seeing out.

- Rehabilitation Pod is zoning soft. It's designed on an RV platform and can be placed in ninety percent of the municipalities in the U.S. It can be leased at a lower cost and outfitted for extended care or short term rehab.

- MEDCottage Classic, available only in Virginia, comes as a kit for the homeowner to assemble themselves or hire a local contractor for installation.

FabCab

FabCab's expertise draws from years of following changing age demographics and a passion for designing "inclusive" homes that enable people to thrive regardless of their age or ability. Universal Design principles are woven into everything they do and they are dedicated to designing aesthetically pleasing, friendly, inspiring spaces for people to live active lifestyles.

Due to the rapidly increasing number of older adults combined with current economic conditions, including the skyrocketing costs of retirement healthcare facilities and erratic home values, housing options are necessary that allow seniors to remain cost conscious while they look for options to stay independent and age in place.

FabCab designs and sells pre-fabricated environmentally-friendly homes and accessory dwelling units (ADUs). They strive to lead the market specializing in design for all ages and environmentally sustainable design by providing clients eco-friendly and universally designed cabins that support healthy lifestyles. FabCab prides itself on prefabricated housing that doesn't look boxy or "pieced together." The integration of timber framing allows more room for design flexibility.

ADUs are small structures built on residential lots, as an accessory use to the primary dwelling unit. Due to growing demand for this type of flexible housing option, many municipalities are making changes to zoning laws and permitting requirements to allow or even encourage ADU use.

FabCab uses include a guest house, home office, writer's or artist's studio, caregiver's residence, in-law apartment, rental unit or a cabin on a vacation property. Their two main designs are TimberCab and ModCab homes.

TimberCab homes feature Douglas Fir timberframes as well as the highest level of finish. The timberframes and wall/roof panels are pre-cut with state of the art technology and labeled for an efficient build at the site by a licensed contractor.

ModCab homes feature a structural insulated panel (SIP) shell as well as a standard level of interior finish. They are available with either a shed roof or a modern gable roof. The structural shell is pre-cut off site with state of the art technology and labeled for an efficient build at the site by a licensed contractor.

Both models can be shipped to most building sites due to the flexibility of their home packages.

FabCab's approach to sustainability is simple. They design healthy, efficient environments to accommodate peoples' varied lifestyles. They are equally passionate about designing a space that is usable for people with a range of ages and abilities, as they are dedicated to offering clients eco-friendly and economically resourceful spaces.

FabCab takes advantage of the trend to emphasize quality rather than quantity. External options that can be added include a green roof, solar (hot water or photovoltaic), geothermal options, and rainwater collection systems.

FabCab benefits:

- Efficient design: An open plan and efficient layout maximizes floor space.

- Renewable resources: The timber frame line uses renewable/ sustainably harvested Douglas Fir, using less wood than stud framing.

- Less waste: State of the art, computerized cutting machines minimize waste. This creates precise, high quality assemblies, and reduces time delays.

- Less transportation: With either product line, the materials are brought to the site in fewer shipments than with typical construction.

- Energy efficiency: The structural insulated panels (SIPS) walls are extremely energy efficient. Plumbing lines can be built in for optional solar water heaters on the roof and high efficiency hot water heaters will power a radiant floor heating system.

- Healthy indoor air quality: Low VOC paints and finishes are used throughout the cabins. An anti-microbial glaze on tiles and fixtures reduce the potential for bacteria growth in the bathroom.

- Water efficiency: State of the art water efficient plumbing fixtures by TOTO reduce the margin consumption of water. Optional cisterns can catch and store rainwater from the roof.

- Recycled materials: Green materials and components with a high degree of recycled content are used throughout FabCab's products.

- Less commuting: In many cases, ADUs are placed in neighborhoods which are close to amenities, so that the occupants may have short distances to travel to frequently-visited locations. Home offices and studios greatly decrease commutes.

- Higher density: With more housing options for people to live near to employment areas, there is less pressure to develop valuable green space in more remote areas.

THE HOME STORE

In business since 1986, The Home Store has been one

of the largest custom modular home builders in Massachusetts, Connecticut, Rhode Island, New Hampshire, Vermont, New York, Long Island, and New Jersey. They offer over 450 house floor plans for custom modular homes, any of which can meet Universal Design and Energy Star requirements.

The Home Store's core business is modular home sales on a scattered lot basis. Typically, its customers use The Home Store to build a custom designed home on a lot they have purchased in the community of their choice.

As a leader and innovator in modular home design and construction, The Home Store has built everything from two-story models to large scale homes up to 2,500 square feet. Upscale amenities in some of their models have included vaulted foyers with wrap-around oak railings, a jade-green marble fireplace surrounded by wall-to-wall custom oak bookcases, and a first-floor living area finished in 6-panel oak doors with oak casings, crown moldings, and chair rail.

In 1994 The Home Store joined with Ron Mace, Director for Universal Design at North Carolina State University, to launch a new line of affordable modular homes, called the Universal Home Series. Mace's designs are based on the principle that homes should be usable by all people, regardless of their age, size, abilities, or disabilities. It is this line that appeals to the growing number of elderly and aging baby boomers who discover that their homes are ill-equipped to meet their changing needs and circumstances.

The Home Store President, Andy Gianino, is the author of *The Modular Home* a comprehensive handbook for prospective modular home buyers. The book contains everything prospective buyers should know about buying and building a modular home or adding a "granny pod" type modular home to an existing property, including choosing dealers, working with general contractors, selecting floor plans, choosing details, financing construction, and more.

Granny pods do offer an affordable home choice for individuals who can't shoulder the financial burden of traditional assisted living communities. For example, NextDoor Housing's granny pods usually sell for around $45,000. Compare that to the average cost for living just one year in a Minnesota assisted living community of $40,000.

Interestingly, Minnesota is one of the more affordable states for assisted living. At the top end is New Jersey, where a one-bedroom apartment will set a resident back about $6,500 per month on average, according to Lincoln Financial Group's WhatCareCosts.com website. Designed to assist financial advisors in helping clients plan long-term care needs, WhatCareCosts.com is an eye-opener when it comes to current costs in different areas of the country as well as for cost projections well into the future.

The national average for a one-bedroom assisted living apartment is $4,560 per month, up from last year's $4,383. Below you'll see the most expensive and least expensive states for assisted living.

Most Expensive

1. New Jersey, $6,587 per month

2. Massachusetts, $6,323 per month

3. Connecticut, $6,091 per month

4. Maryland, $6,005 per month

5. Maine, $5,928 per month

Least Expensive

1. North Dakota, $3,102 per month

2. Mississippi, $3,327 per month

3. Louisiana, $3,455 per month

4. Alabama, $3,536 per month

5. Arkansas, $3,653 per month

Let's look at some of the more traditional senior living options available in most communities.

SENIOR APARTMENTS

Senior apartments or age restricted communities may be market-rate, multi-family residential rental properties or even mobile home villages where occupancy is restricted to at least 80% of adults aged 55 years or older. Although optional meal plans may be offered, these properties typically offer self-contained units with no central kitchen facilities or meal provisions, differentiating senior apartments from independent living units. Community rooms, social activities, and other amenities may be provided.

INDEPENDENT LIVING (IL)

Independent living (IL) provides a bridge between senior apartments and assisted living properties. As part of a monthly fee or rental rate, IL boasts several services such as housekeeping and linen, transportation, social and recreational activities, and access to some or all daily meals through a central kitchen/dining facility. To be truly considered an IL community, the community must boast a minimum of one common dining facility and provide at least one daily meal for the monthly fee. IL properties generally are best for seniors who need little (if any) assistance with Activities of Daily Living (ADL). Typically these units are not licensed for health care and offer no skilled nursing beds. Residents requiring extra assistance may access home health care services from an outside agency or through a partner of the property's management company.

ASSISTED LIVING (AL)

Assisted living (AL) properties are regulated by the state and provide a greater level of care than IL. Most AL residences will offer everything an IL community does, but in addition supportive care from trained employees is available in the majority of the units, which may or may not be offered in a separate wing, floor or building. For those unable to live totally independently, assistance with ADLs, including medication management, bathing, dressing, toileting, ambulating, and eating is provided.

The key phrase in the foregoing sentence is "unable to live totally independently." Assistance should not be confused with continuous skilled nursing care. While this type of property may have some nursing beds as well as some wings or floors dedicated to memory care, the majority are licensed for AL.

SKILLED NURSING

Skilled nursing facilities are licensed daily rate or rental properties in which most of the residents require round-the-clock nursing or medical care. Most of these facilities are licensed for Medicare/Medicaid reimbursement and may include minimal AL or Memory Care units.

CONTINUING CARE RETIREMENT COMMUNITIES (CCRCs)

Continuing care retirement communities (CCRCs) combine IL, AL and skilled nursing to provide a continuum of care on a single campus. Required fees vary and may include an entrance fee, condo fee, etc. Most of the units in a CCRC are not licensed skilled nursing beds.

The table on the following page illustrates some of the differences among senior living options.

	Senior Apartment	Independent Living	Assisted Living	Skilled Nursing Facilities	CCRCs and Combinations
State Licensing	Not required	Not required	Required	Required	Required
State Approval Needed to Build	Not required	Not required	Not in most states, but there are a few with CON requirements	Most states require a CON or application for Medicaid funding	Most states have some state approval requirements
Resident Funding	Private pay or section 8. Many have low income housing tax credits and have rent and income restrictions	Private pay	Primarily private pay, some Medicaid waiver	Predominantly funded by Medicaid and Medicare	Primarily private pay, some Medicaid/ Medicare in assisted and/ or nursing components
Payment Type	Primarily rent by the month	About ¾ rental by the month, ¼ entry fee	Primarily rent by the month, a small percentage are entry fee	Primarily rent by the day, virtually none are entry fee	Most require an entry fee for IL and some for AL as well
Typical Size	60 to 250 units. Average is +/-200 units	80 to 200 units. Average is +/-135 units	40 to 100 units. Average is +/-90 units	100 to 200 beds. Average is +/-120 beds.	Typically 200+ units/ beds; many are in the 300 to 500 range.
Meal Service	Limited	Typically 1 to 3 meals per day included in rent	Typically 3 meals per day included in rent	Typically 3 meals per day included in rent	Varies by care types within the community
Amenities	Transportation and activities	All provided in senior apartments, plus meal service, housekeeping and 24-hour monitoring	All provided in IL plus laundry and assistance with activities of daily living	All provided in AL plus 24-hour nursing care	Varies by care types within the community

Source: Seniors Housing Industry Outlook published by IRR Senior Housing & Health Care

THE SENIOR LIVING VALUE PROPOSITION

Regardless of which segment within the landscape of senior living choices that retirees consider or select, the focus will be on which one provides the greatest value proposition. A lackluster economy has placed a significant burden on seniors, which indirectly impacts senior living communities. The recent recession placed personal savings in the crosshairs. Home values plummeted and only recently have begun to recover. Coupled with increased costs of living, these factors combined have done their part in shrinking the overall net worth of today's senior.

According to a report by the Insured Retirement Institute, just 24 percent of baby boomers feel confident that their savings will last throughout their retirement years. Only 55 percent have retirement savings at all. Of those who have something socked away, nearly half have less than $100,000, a figure that would generate less than $7,000 annually in retirement income. About 20% fear not having enough savings to cover basic living expenses.

If you include Social Security income of, say, $12,000 to $15,000 annually, that equates to an income just above the federal minimum wage – about $10 per hour – if the person worked full time.

For those people, some of whom always imagined that a senior living community would be in their future, they are now faced with cohabiting with children or other family members in order to save money and share expenses.

Intensified competition among senior living communities will require new and innovative methods of maintaining census. In order to compete against similar communities and present a viable choice for prospective residents, senior living communities must look for ways to reduce costs. Discounted entry fees, more affordable housing options and/or "cafeteria-type" amenities may provide the choice and value necessary for seniors to take the plunge. Allowing seniors to select from a variety of options, some customized especially for them, addresses the need for choice and value as well as convenience.

LUXURY SENIOR LIVING

The one exception to the value for dollars mantra is the

niche market for luxury senior living. Several developers have moved into the luxury senior living niche. Of the 10,000 Baby Boomers retiring daily, a certain segment has plenty of money to spend.

The Baby Boomer generation is reported to be the richest ever with $3 trillion in net worth. One wealth management company has actually forecasted that this group will hold $54 trillion in assets by 2030 when it will start to pass away in large numbers.

Whatever way you slice it, that's a chunk of change. Several developers are banking on the fact that those who have the "gold" during their golden years will spend it to live luxuriously.

For these individuals, luxury senior living stands as a well-deserved reward for those who worked hard (and successfully) all their lives and who expect to play hard during their best years yet to come. They seek world-class dining and deluxe amenities they have earned the right to enjoy.

A large share of senior housing projects in development fall into the luxury unit category. The REITs that are pursuing these properties are trading at initial yields in the 6% to 6.5% range in primary markets. In more secondary locations, these units can trend upward of 100 basis points.

Despite the fact that most of the luxury senior developments build in 10 primary markets, the markets in question have a history of stable economic outlooks and strong absorption trends, laying to rest significant fears of potential overbuilding.

By the end of 2016, the average rent for IL units was expected to rise 3% year over year, besting $3,000 monthly for the first time. At the same time, IL occupancy is expected to reach 91.7%, holding steady from the same time in 2015 as supply side pressure increases in some markets.

AL average rents remain robust and continue to rise, despite some downward pressure on occupancy and higher completions. In the past year, average rents rose 2.7% to $4,401 per month. The luxury AL units being completed in the coming months should keep rents moving up.

Despite the economically challenged and comfortable, a large mid-range contingent of seniors is seeking some balance between quality and affordability and the developers who satisfy that need will have a large pool of potential customers.

THE POTENTIAL ROLE FOR GOVERNMENT

Government involvement in the senior living industry will likely continue to grow in direct proportion to the age of voters (seniors over younger generations). Expect increased spending to drive the industry's move toward upgraded facilities and services. Older voters will pressure the government to upgrade facilities and possibly fund senior social programs.

However, greater involvement on the part of government will also require greater accountability and transparency from the industry itself. Government intervention almost always brings with it public policy and regulation. An increased demand for accountability could force communities to meet certain governmental standards as the politicos cast a more discerning eye and take a renewed interest in the industry. Expect some "value added" programs like health and wellness to become requirements as opposed to options.

Industry participants have long predicted that governmental regulation will be a top issue in determining what the future of senior living will look like. Also greater transparency on pricing and review sites will lead to more informed seniors who can differentiate the varied programs and communities available.

SENIOR LIVING REINVENTED

Senior living, like so many other industries, is moving from a service delivery model to an experience delivery model (discussed in greater detail in "Chapter 9: The Resident Experience"). Communities that maintain the status quo are set to lose market share and pricing power to the new senior living trailblazers. A judicious examination of existing services and an openness to a reframed offering that emphasizes experience design and delivery in a holistic resident lifestyle will be the new standard against which communities will be evaluated. Those in the industry who also pay close attention to the current demographic and psychographic climate – longer life expectancy, greater diversity, increased interest in health and wellness, greater facility with technology, and higher expectation levels – have an opportunity to craft the new resident experience ahead of the curve and ahead of the competition.

Having put the industry in context and the challenges facing senior living communities today, I share the current unit makeup and distribution of one of Tuscan Gardens' newest developments, Tuscan Gardens of Delray Beach.

TUSCAN GARDENS OF DELRAY BEACH

- **116 Units**

- **144 Beds**

- **12 Independent Living Units/12 Beds**

- **64 Assisted Living Units/78 Beds**

- **40 Memory Care Units/54 Beds**

- **132,000 Square Feet**

Supportive Independent Living

- (4) 2 Bedroom / 2 Bathroom Units at 950 Sq. Ft. each

- (4) 2 Bedroom / 1 Bathroom Units at 875 Sq. Ft. each

- (4) 1 Bedroom / 1 Bathroom Units at 700 Sq. Ft. each

Assisted Living: 3-Story Building

- (10) 2 Bedroom / 2 Bathroom Units at 875 Sq. Ft. each

- (14) 2 Bedroom / 1 Bathroom Units at 775 Sq. Ft. each

- (34) 1 Bedroom / 1 Bathroom Units at 625 Sq. Ft. each

- (6) Petite Bedroom / 1 Bathroom Units at 450 Sq. Ft. each

Memory Care: 2-Story Building

- (26) Private Memory Care Studio at 300 Sq. Ft. each

- (14) 2 Bedroom / 1 Bathroom Units at 450 Sq. Ft. each

Different management and operational styles certainly impact the state of senior living today. However, with regard to management and operation, rather than discuss the advantages and disadvantages to the self-operated or contract models (covered in "Chapter 14: Management Systems"), I thought it might be most beneficial to discuss my own management philosophies and those that guide the operation of Tuscan Gardens. This will be shared in great detail, particularly in regard to staffing, in "Chapter 13: Creating Community, Conversation & Culture".

HIGHLIGHTS

1. Niche communities catering to individuals of certain faiths, professions, ethnicities, interests, sexuality, education, religions or lifestyles are becoming more popular.

2. UBRCs, a subset of niche communities, are connected to colleges and universities and ensure access to enriching educational experiences.

3. The Aging in Place initiative may be helped with the creation of "granny pods" or other units that can be placed on a family member's property.

4. Traditional senior housing options run the gamut of size, price, and amenities.

5. While luxury senior living is a category that is gaining ground, mid-range developers will have the largest pool of potential residents.

6. The new trailblazers in senior living will be those promoting a reframed offering that emphasizes experience, design, and delivery in a holistic resident lifestyle.

CHAPTER 3

THE CASE FOR COMMUNITY

The closest thing to being cared for is to care for someone else.
~ Carson McCullers

As mentioned in the "Preface," the concept of putting my mother into a senior living community or some sort of "home" was culturally taboo. However, after my father passed away and as my mother's health issues began to require a greater level of care, it became necessary to at least entertain the idea of, well, *something.*

What that something would be needed time to take shape. We discussed the advantages and disadvantages of Mom moving in with one of us, using home health care services, engaging private live-in caregivers or applying for residency at any one of the myriad senior living communities in the area. Each had its good points, but conversely each also had drawbacks and deciding which negatives we could live with as a family became the main concern.

Living with one of us (my sister or myself) simply wasn't a workable solution. Neither of our homes was outfitted properly for Mom's needs and the necessary modifications were prohibitive from the standpoint of both time and money. Plus, Mom needed someone available to her, if not 24/7, certainly a lion's share of the day. The businesses in which my wife, Janet, and I were involved required us to travel frequently, as well as devote full business days during the work week, which kept us from being the choice for full-time caregiver.

So, to begin our journey, we chose to explore a home health care service in which a caregiver would come in for a portion of the day to assist Mom with her needs. However, it became clear that this would be unworkable almost from the start. The "turnstile" which is today's home health care service worker made this an untenable arrangement. No sooner did Mom learn a caregiver's name than the person disappeared from her life and a new face crossed the threshold. With no fundamental learning about Mom – her history, her family, her likes and dislikes – there was no basis for bonding or rapport. A veritable stranger came to the door every other day, often to assist her with the most private and intimate needs. The situation was uncomfortable for Mom, if not downright confusing.

Next, we thought we should explore senior living communities in the area. My sister, Joy, vetted several and then passed on the names of the ones she thought were possibilities. Joy's requirements were stringent and she didn't pass on many names. But for the ones she did think had promise, I took on the responsibility of visiting them with Mom to get a feel for the atmosphere and amenities.

By this time, Mom wasn't really ambulatory and our "site visits" involved me getting her in her wheelchair and wheeling her into the lobbies. One such visit remains burned in my brain. I remember wheeling Mom through the big glass double doors of what's considered a very popular community here in the Orlando area. We paused just inside the door to take in the surroundings. It was at that moment that Mom looked up at me over her left shoulder, her eyes welling with tears, and said, "La melancholia." You don't need to be fluent in Italian to understand what she was feeling. With that said, I promptly turned the wheelchair 180 degrees and left as quickly as we came.

I knew what Mom meant. There was a distinct melancholy about the place and all I could think at the time was, "So, this is what it all comes down to? This is where her wonderful well-lived life ends?" At that moment, I hadn't even entertained the thought of approaching the senior living industry as a business. All I wanted was for my mother to be cared for in an environment she deserved – of purpose, passion & joy.

These experiments left us with one last option – the least economical, but most appropriate choice for Mom – a private, in-home caregiver. In having a caregiver move into Mom's own home and live with her 24/7, we would be able to provide a continuity of care, continuity of experience and continuity of relationship that Mom needed and deserved.

At that point the Pino family advertised for a live-in caregiver and, happily, we got very lucky with some superb individuals who loved and cared for Mom as if she had been their own parent.

Mom bonded with these women and they shared a meaningful life together. Her caregivers learned to cook authentic Italian food with real ingredients from Mom's own recipes and those moments across the table became some of our most treasured memories. In fact, I still call Sharon Leichering, one of Mom's long-term caregivers, from time to time to clarify some of the finer points on Mom's recipes as she knows them all by heart.

Despite the closeness with her caregivers, living at home did involve compromise. Mom's social circle became an ever-shrinking spiral. Some friends died. Others came less and less frequently due to their own diminishing capabilities and faculties with regard to hearing or vision. Some didn't drive anymore or had their cars taken away. Others went to live with adult children or at senior living communities.

My mother's world went from a vibrant lifestyle where she was out and about all the time with one of her "closest" 400 friends to one confined within her own four walls. Visits became few and far between except for her immediate family. Janet, Joy, our kids, and I visited every weekend, but inevitably the time came for goodbyes and Mom's crestfallen look made me suffer the pang of guilt ever so much more.

Throughout this entire experience with Mom, I wrestled with the question, "Is this really the best option?" The answer, of course, was no. But it was the best in relation to the other alternatives. Nothing else made sense to me.

The private caregiver situation lasted 10 years and the expense was, in a word, exorbitant. Two full-time employees don't come cheap, even considering the fact that you are offering room and board. In fact it seemed that the expense of the options was inversely proportionate to the amount of guilt sustained from making that selection: I suffered financially and emotionally.

Within that decade-long period the recession hit me and my businesses hard. I lost my income for two solid years – from

September 2009 to November 2011. Yet, I continued to support Mom in the manner she found to be the most comfortable and the most comforting. Would it have been wonderful to find an alternative? Yes, but what would it need to look like? And, as I shared in the "Preface," that became for me the seminal moment.

From my experience with Mom, I knew what it *didn't* look like. My own research showed that the type of place for my mom didn't exist – at least not close by. So, I had no choice but to create it.

That was the driver. Then the question became, "Could this be a real business?" I hadn't been looking at it as a business, but at its most basic a business addresses an unfulfilled need in the marketplace and seeks to fill it. The Pino family was proof positive there was a need in the marketplace. If that's the case, there would have to be people like me who would not be prepared to patronize the senior living communities currently on the market. However, if they had the type of place I envisioned, maybe they would. Any way you slice it, that's a business opportunity.

My concept of concierge living for seniors then began to take shape with a goal of creating a community that people *want to live in*, rather than *need to live in*. It would be a community like no other community. I wanted to create a place not where people go to die, but a place where people go to live, with everything to live an emotionally and physically satisfying life right there. Nobody wants to give up quality of life simply because they might need age-based assistance from time to time, and nobody should have to.

I believed then, and now, that there is a strong case to be made for creating a community which takes care of all of those needs, yet, one that has broken free of the historical attributes of senior living communities. By reinventing senior living in this way, seniors are offered a safe environment in which they can choose all the wonderful things life still has to offer in an atmosphere of intimacy and elegance.

Happily, since having entered the senior living industry, I have discovered several kindred spirits. It's heartening to see so many colleagues who share my passion for reframing senior living from the stodgy and conventional product it once was to the dynamic and exciting opportunity that it is becoming. I'm grateful to be part of that process with a whole cadre of individuals who are pushing the envelope in terms of lifestyle and amenities.

The foregoing encapsulates my journey to understanding and embracing senior living communities for what they could be, rather than what they were then, with an emphasis on enhancing the positives and ameliorating the negatives.

Of the types of living arrangements for seniors discussed in the previous chapter and above, as mentioned, each has its own specific advantages and disadvantages. While the National Aging in Place Council reports that more than 90 percent of older adults would prefer to age in place, that's not always financially, logistically or emotionally feasible or optimal, particularly as it pertains to loneliness and lack of social interaction.

Author Ralph Villman's book, *And Where Do We Live When We Get Older*, shows the pitfalls of the aging in place movement and that remaining in the family home once an older age is reached is not always a desirable option. Ralph's book covers all of the traditional senior living options as well as some widely known alternative senior living arrangements.

Regardless of which option you and your family members ultimately choose, to have a meaningful and vibrant lifestyle at any age, what we are calling for our purposes *The Art of Living*, several factors must be in place:

- *Environment:* The components of a comfortable life including maintenance elements such as lighting and temperature to the more aesthetic considerations of well-designed and decorated rooms.

- *Ease:* A lack of obstacles in everyday life to allow the efficient conduct of normal activities. Often, diminished physical or mental capacity may affect the ease with which many seniors live their lives. However, assistive technologies and environmental modification can overcome these issues and lead to an enhanced enjoyment of life.

- *Self-actualization:* The ability to continue learning on a lifelong basis, self-actualization refers to personal growth and progress. Taking classes to learn new skills or reinforce current skills provides seniors with a sense of achievement. A wide variety of activities ensures that there is always something new to learn.

- *Recognition:* To continually feel valued for achievements or contributions helps seniors feel worthwhile in their social circle or community. Whether it's knitting hats for the local crisis nursery or playing piano during happy hour, giving back in some small way feeds the soul.

- *Health and wellness:* If self-actualization feeds the mind and the emotions, health and wellness serves the body. From good eating habits to regular physical activity, whole body health infuses the retirement years with vitality and verve.

- *Social interaction:* Social interaction in all its forms strengthens the bonds between individuals. By facilitating access to entertainment, activities and events, you set the stage for close interaction between residents and staff. Social interaction doesn't necessarily need to be a scheduled event. It can be as simple as chatting over coffee and croissants or greeting others during a stroll through the grounds.

According to the Organisation for Economic Cooperation and Development (OECD), a group dedicated to promoting policies that improve the economic and social wellbeing of people around the world, the proportion of the population aged 80 or greater is predicted to increase to almost 10% by 2050. These older individuals will require several intangibles to be present in their day to day activities in order to reach a meaningful quality of life: choice, autonomy, dignity, individuality, comfort, wellbeing, security and social contact. Perhaps no other type of senior living option is as well equipped to deliver the final component – social interaction– than senior living communities.

To understand the topic of loneliness vs. social interaction, it's helpful to break it down into three distinct components: an individual's emotional state, interactions with caregivers and technological advancements.

EMOTIONAL STATE

An individual's emotional state establishes the number and intensity of quality relationships required to combat loneliness.

Therefore, some people may have fewer relationships than they consider desirable. Others may feel that an adequate number of relationships hasn't reached the depth of intimacy preferred. In either case, the person would characterize this lacking in personal relationships as loneliness.

One of the more popular metrics used by scholars in this area is the UCLA Loneliness Scale. Through a series of direct questions, the scale evaluates how often the subject of the assessment feels in certain ways in relation to others. Some sample questions from the UCLA Loneliness Scale include:

- How often do you feel that you lack companionship?

- How often do you feel that there is no one you can turn to?

- How often do you feel alone?

- How often do you feel that you are no longer close to anyone?

- How often do you feel that your interests and ideas are not shared by those around you?

- How often do you feel that you are "in tune" with the people around you?

- How often do you feel left out?

- How often do you feel that your relationships with others are not meaningful?

- How often do you feel that no one really knows you well?

- How often do you feel isolated from others?

- How often do you feel shy?

- How often do you feel that people are around you but not with you?

Loneliness tends to be categorized by a lack of

"connectedness" in three increasingly intimate settings. Collective connectedness refers to belonging in groups with which an individual feels a sense of identification. Relational connectedness is the closeness felt through friendships, social relationships, and confidants. Intimate connectedness describes family or romantic relationships.

It's not unusual that seniors might feel a lack of intimate or relational connectedness. Spouses and friends pass away and younger family members have their own busy lives to lead. Collective connectedness is certainly something that the right senior living community can provide and with proper training caregivers at a community can provide a type of relational connectedness. Either of these could lead to intimate connectedness with others at the community.

Loneliness can also impact other areas of seniors' lives including health (poor sleeping and eating habits, substance abuse, mental illness, depression, and suicide) and financial well-being (a tendency to spend to fill the void in one's life).

Furthermore, loneliness can also be exacerbated by cross cultural or language differences that can exist in senior living environments. Understanding elements of daily activities where cultural or language gaps can be accommodated will do its part to mitigate loneliness.

Eliminating loneliness and enhancing emotional vitality helps seniors maintain a positive outlook on life and an optimistic view of the future. In a study of 884 older adults, University of Michigan psychologists found that the seniors who scored higher on perceived control of important aspects of their lives – community involvement, hobbies or family connections – were more likely to be alive at the study's six and seven year follow-ups.

INTERACTIONS WITH CAREGIVERS

Emotions that are connected to loneliness with which trained caregivers in a senior living environment have the opportunity to impact include the following:

- *Aggression:* Aggression rises when seniors have lost the ability to perform many of their activities of daily living. This can lead to isolation and self-criticism. Caregivers trained to support autonomy provide choice whenever possible, allowing seniors to do or have what they want within an adapted environment rather than doing or having what they are told. This is particularly important in the areas of food and activities.

Everyone experiences some type of physical change, whether severe or mild, due to aging. What makes us who we are remains relatively unchanged, except in situations of cognitive problems. In some care settings, the primary driver is safety that leads to overprotection in which autonomy is unnecessarily diminished due to reduction in participation in meaningful activities such as hobbies or even basic daily activities.

Interestingly, as autonomy diminishes through continuing physical or mental impairment, feelings of belonging and being part of society (which come more easily in smaller environments that are less institutional) become more important to individuals' self-image. Sensitive caregivers assist seniors with this transition.

• *Fear:* Unfamiliar environments, such as admission to a senior living community, can lead to anxiety which amplifies loneliness. Some people cope with fear by withdrawing; others reach out, almost desperately to anyone who will listen. When not properly dealt with, fear can lead to pessimism and fatigue. The handling of fear may also be influenced by cultural heritage: the more gregarious Latino or African cultures transition better than Anglos, for example.

Caregivers looking to combat fear and its associated consequences have two powerful tools at their disposal: *gratitude and hope.* Coaching seniors to feel gratitude for the level of connectedness that they do have is an integral part of eliminating fear. This is particularly helpful in the evening, when reflecting on the daily activities and the opportunities for social interaction. Expressing gratitude for their accomplishments during the day (however diminished they may be from those of their younger self) sets the stage for a more fulfilling life. In other words, gratitude feeds on itself.

Hope moves people through challenging events. It can be nurtured through faith, life or social support groups.

The presence of compassionate and empathetic caregivers is the primary advantage of senior living communities over aging in place. Compassion motivates individuals to help those in need. In health care research on the impact of authentic human relationships between patients and care givers, bedside manner has been found to have a greater impact than cholesterol-lowering drugs on high cardiac risk patients.

- *Empathy:* This is best demonstrated with caregivers who ask the right questions of those in need. It includes asking residents about social interaction hopes and needs beyond the provision of daily activities (such as dressing, eating, bathing etc.) and connecting them to potential solutions.

Caregivers are the true unsung heroes in senior living settings and the demand for empathetic, compassionate, and hopeful individuals will continue to grow, particularly in light of the following trends.

- **Increased longevity and lifespan**

- **More women (historically the unpaid, family-based caregiver) in the workforce**

- **Fewer multi-generational households**

- **Greater single person households**

- **Increased need for multi-dimensional care beyond the basic daily needs that a family member may be comfortable providing**

Fewer and fewer people filling the family-based care model shifts greater demand on "professional caregivers." Plus, the definition of caregiver can and should be expanded to include all of the individuals who impact a senior's life, such as facility maintenance staff, housekeepers, dining staff, receptionists, and drivers to name a few.

While these service workers are neither clinically trained nor family members, they are participants in the care continuum and contribute to a senior's quality of life and social interaction. Training service workers in basic listening and interacting skills pays big dividends in increased resident satisfaction. That's because these types of workers are often seen as safe or non-threatening. Seniors feel comfortable in confiding in a housekeeper, sometimes even more so than in true clinical workers.

Role modeling within the team – having one team member play resident while the other performs his or her job duties – develops empathy and shows how meaningful a simple smile or hello can be to a new resident who feels fear or trepidation in the new environment.

Interestingly, as the exchanges between team members and residents grow and develop, team members typically begin to go above and beyond. They feel differently about the residents. Trust begets trust and team members feel that the residents have given them permission to be friends.

Caregivers, too, have their own issues with feelings of loneliness and need for social interaction. In a community setting, caregivers have an opportunity to bond with each other, over a break room coffee for example. Private caregivers, on the other hand, frequently feel isolated and alone. As you can see, making connections with others who understand their experiences and feelings isn't reserved for seniors only.

TECHNOLOGY

While we deal more comprehensively with the subject of technology in a later chapter, the topic should be touched upon here with regard to its ability to either isolate or connect people.

Many people expect robots to be the future of elder care as we move into the perfect storm of 1.5 billion people over the age of 65 by 2050 and a dearth of trained and willing caregivers to feed, dress, and medicate them.

As we looked forward to robotics changing the way senior

care is delivered, many people worried about the lack of human interaction and how that would impact the elderly. Now, with the advent of tablet technology, smartphones and other devices, many people seem quite content interacting with avatars over humans. As this technology progresses and comes into common usage, it will be interesting to see how seniors interact with the technological devices and whether they ultimately exacerbate or ameliorate the sense of loneliness and need for social contact.

The following three principles seem well founded and worth observing in these early days of technological takeover of the senior experience.

- *Establish a human contact foundation.* Technology, robotics, and other mechanical advancements do a better job in a supportive role rather than as a primary contact. Let humans lay the groundwork and establish rapport and social interaction. Then, technology can overcome time and distance in perpetuating the relationship. Connectivity, however, should be tempered with human activity and interaction. It's easy to become dependent on electronic connections (e.g., Facebook, Twitter) and experience a sense of loss or boredom in their absence.

- *Gather and use data wisely.* Technology, in general, is a glorified form of data gathering and storage. It can learn everything about a person if someone desires to feed it that information. However, unlike human relationships, greater levels of information don't lead to greater intimacy. In other words, I am closer to my cousin than I am to the person who works in the office suite next to mine, in part because I have much more information (and personal experience, of course) about him as opposed to the individual in my office building whom I see in the elevator. Technology can gather information, but it cannot (as yet) relate to that information on a deep level. Caregivers gather information by listening intently and seeking to know the other person.

- *"Low-tech" still has a role to play.* Our fixation on high-tech devices and connectivity can often make us lose sight of what technology doesn't do well. Through virtual reality, it's possible to stroll through the gardens of Versailles. However, through my own two feet (or wheelchair or walker), I can stroll through the vegetable patch at Tuscan Gardens, for example. Yes, you can have dinner with your best friend via Facetime, but isn't it better to have dinner across the table? Allow technology to enhance life, not to replace life.

Having seen how older adults are at risk for loneliness and isolation, it's obvious that senior living communities are best equipped to provide the necessary aspects for a life well lived. Engaged caregivers and programmatic elements keep loneliness at bay. Technology has a role to play, but not at the expense of day to day human interaction.

In the following chapters, I'll examine how the environment and resident lifestyle can be reinvented to embrace the best in interior and exterior elements, while designing a vibrant lifestyle that makes *The Art of Living* a lifelong journey. Along the way, I'll call out several trendsetting communities and individuals who are leading the charge to reinvent senior living in motivating and meaningful ways.

HIGHLIGHTS

1. Six factors should be present at any senior living community to ensure the best opportunity for an exceptional quality of life: Environment, Ease, Self-Actualization, Recognition, Health and Wellness, and Social Interaction.

2. The environment created by a professional senior living community is perhaps best suited for combating the loneliness to which many seniors are predisposed.

3. Professional, properly trained caregivers are best equipped to deal with the emotions seniors experience arising out of loneliness, including aggression and fear.

4. Role playing allows caregivers to develop empathy and shows how meaningful a simple smile or hello can be to a new resident.

5. With the predicted dearth of trained and willing caregivers in the near future, technology will have to be leveraged to feed, dress, and medicate the estimated 1.5 billion people over the age of 65 by 2050.

6. While technology has a role to play in the new senior living frontier, it should be deployed with a large measure of human interaction.

CHAPTER 4

SENIOR LIVING PAY MODELS

Retirement is like a long vacation in Las Vegas. The goal is to enjoy it the fullest, but not so fully that you run out of money.
~ Jonathan Clements

If, as conjectured in the previous chapter, community living represents one of the best options for today's senior due to the presence of environment, ease, self-actualization, recognition, health and wellness, and social interaction, the question becomes how much does this meaningful and vibrant lifestyle cost and how does one pay for it?

Many individuals fail to consider these costs in their long-term plans. Some believe they will be hale and hearty enough to "age in place," thereby allowing them to preserve their assets for their heirs. Others think government subsidies will cover any senior living needs they have.

Just because someone hasn't planned doesn't mean they will not be able to secure appropriate care. It just means their choices may be limited to a selection that doesn't offer the setting, style or amenities they would prefer.

Often the sheer cost of senior living (particularly the higher levels of care) takes prospective residents and their families by surprise. A situation exacerbated by many communities' reluctance to share pricing information online. Cost transparency will continue to be a hot topic in the industry. According to Louisville, Kentucky-based consultancy Conversation Research Institute (CRI), 44% of negative online conversations about assisted living involves finances.

- CRI analyzed conversations about senior living contained in news sites, comments sections, social networks, blogs, review sites, forums, and more from November 1, 2015 to October 31, 2016. In doing so, CRI discovered that cost is of great concern for buyers looking into assisted living communities, more so than for independent living or skilled nursing. A fact senior living communities might do well to heed.

Of special note, too, is financing or funding in the case of a prospective resident who needs Memory Care, which can quickly and easily bankrupt a family. Because this is such an important issue, I highly recommend a book like *The 36 Hour Day* by Peter Rabins and Nancy Mace. Originally published in 1981 with five subsequent editions, this definitive guide on all matters related to dementia contains valuable information on appropriate living arrangements for seniors with dementia and various ways to fund that care.

In general, seniors use private pay, financial assistance, insurance, or some combination of the three.

PRIVATE PAY

Typically, potential senior living residents and their families fund community costs through private financial sources. Some individuals have health insurance programs or senior living care insurance policies that may reimburse some costs. Alternatively, a number of communities may also have financial assistance programs available for prospective residents.

When it comes to private financial sources, the primary residence represents most seniors' largest asset. Many seniors sell or rent their homes to pay for senior living in whole or in part. The drawback to selling a home to fund senior living is that, depending on the sales price, sooner or later the proceeds will be exhausted.

With regard to leasing your home and using the rental payments for senior living, chances are that the gap between rent and senior living fees will be significant. Considering that the average residential rental rate in the United States is approximately $1,000 per month, that represents a shortfall of between $2,000 and $3,000 for the average monthly assisted living fee.

According to a report by the Harvard Joint Center for

Housing Studies, if a homeowner taps into their home equity, either by selling outright or obtaining a home equity line of credit, they can afford to live for approximately 74 months in an assisted living facility.

For seniors who aren't homeowners or who hope to use only savings or other non-home equity resources to pay for assisted living, the situation is a bit more bleak. It's estimated they will only be able to pay for 29 months in a facility. The typical older homeowner has 42 times more wealth than the typical older renter, meaning renters would only be able to afford two months of assisted living.

Reverse mortgages are another option, but care should be taken to fully understand this funding method. Reverse mortgages are available to homeowners 62 years or older, allowing them to convert part of their home equity into cash. This type of mortgage tends to appeal because it doesn't require the senior to give up the home altogether. Rather, the homeowner may receive a lump sum or monthly payment, which can then be used to pay for long-term care or senior living.

Reverse mortgages were created to allow seniors with limited income to use the accumulated equity in their homes to pay for monthly living expenses or healthcare. However, the proceeds can be used for virtually anything with no restrictions.

These loans are called reverse mortgages because the lender makes payments to you rather than the other way around.

Again, this type of funding should be investigated very carefully. Usually, the borrower is not required to pay back the loan until the home is sold or otherwise vacated. As long as the home is the borrower's primary residence, he or she is not required to make any monthly payments toward the loan balance. The borrower must keep property taxes, homeowners insurance and any homeowner association dues current.

Because of the guidelines that the property unfortunately remain the borrower's primary residence, seniors typically use this type of loan to cover long-term or rehab care in which they will ultimately return to the residence. For those wanting to permanently reside in a senior community, an outright sale is probably a better idea. In any case, experts suggest reverse mortgages be considered only for the last five years or so of an individual's projected life.

FINANCIAL ASSISTANCE

Senior housing may also be funded through various government subsidies. However, seniors should realize that assistance amounts are limited and seniors are restricted on the type of care received and facilities used for receiving that care.

- **Medicare:** Neither Medicare Parts A nor B offer coverage for comprehensive ongoing long-term care. Medicare A (hospital insurance) may cover costs for a semiprivate room, meals, nursing and rehab services, medications, and medical supplies in a skilled nursing facility for the first 100 days post-release from a hospital for an acute illness or injury. Medicare covers the first 20 days at 80%. The remaining time is covered at decreasing rates. Private rooms and services in an assisted living community are *never* covered. Medicare B only offers reimbursement for covered services you receive from a doctor.

- **Medicaid:** Medicaid provides federal health-care assistance to low-income Americans. Medicaid also is the biggest payer for room, board, nursing care, and social activities in nursing homes. Many, but not all, states now cover some assisted living services under their Medicaid programs. Realize, though, that the programs vary widely in terms of coverage amount and eligibility requirements. The Senior Assisted Housing Waiver provides eligible low-income adults a choice of receiving senior living care services in a community-based setting rather than in a nursing facility. Unfortunately, many of these programs may be cut, rather than expanded, due to severe budget deficits in several states.

- **Housing and Veteran Subsidies:** Seniors with annual incomes under $12,000 may qualify for U.S. Department of Housing and Urban Development 202 and Section 8 senior housing, which provide rent subsidies that can help pay for the room-and-board portion of both independent living and assisted living environments. The Department of Veterans Affairs also provides some skilled and intermediate-level care to veterans in its own residences, depending on space availability. Visit http://www1.va.gov/opa/publications/ benefits_book.asp for more information on benefits available to veterans and dependents.

- **Life Care Funding:** Life Care Funding was the first company of its kind to pioneer the concept of converting a life insurance policy into a Long-Term Care Benefit Plan to cover the costs of senior housing and long-term care. By converting the death benefit of an in-force life insurance policy into a long-term care benefit, seniors may be able to cover the costs of skilled nursing home care, assisted living, home health care, and hospice. Life Care Funding has built a network of agents, attorneys, and over 5,000 Homecare, Assisted Living and Nursing Home companies that offer the Life Care Funding program across the United States.

LONG-TERM CARE INSURANCE

Long considered the best way to ensure you can privately fund the type of senior living arrangement you want, the right long-term care policy ensures you will have the greatest choice of housing type (independent living, assisted living and more) in the community of your choice.

Unfortunately, long-term care insurance does have one rather severe catch-22. If you don't have it already, you are probably too late to the party. Individuals interested in this type of insurance should begin doing their homework in their 40s and have a plan in place before age 50.

If you are over age 50 (but younger than 85 when most insurers decline to cover you), expect to pay more. Adult children who may be in a position of caring for elderly parents in their golden years may see helping with higher premiums now to be a better tradeoff than rolling the dice later and paying out of pocket for very expensive care later.

The good news is those same adult children, who may be reading this, are in the perfect position to secure this type of coverage *for themselves* now.

If you are interested in securing long-term care coverage, experts suggest that you:

- Research at least three different companies to compare price and coverage.

- Verify their financial strength through an independent rating system such as AM Best.

- Review their rate history for stability.

- Read the policies carefully, including the fine print.

- Determine if the policy is tax-qualified. If so, premiums may be deductible under medical expenses if you itemize your deductions. Be sure to check with your tax professional.

- Inquire about obtaining an inflation-protected policy, which will ensure sufficient coverage when you file your first claim (whenever that may be).

- Ask questions about anything you don't understand.

Assuming that you've already investigated your pay or financing options for senior living, it's important to understand exactly what you are paying for. You should know that costs vary based on your geographic location, the community profile or amenities, size of living quarters and service level. A basic rate may cover only room (studio, one bedroom or two bedroom) and board (one meal daily or full meal plan) with extra services charged separately. Others may charge a monthly fee that includes everything.

Many communities consider occupancy a "month to month" relationship; others may require a long-term "lease" arrangement.

Research shows that the national median cost for a private one-bedroom apartment in an assisted living community is more than $3,500 per month. Geography has a lot to do with what you'll pay with less expensive areas of the country charging as little as $2,000 monthly and hot spots topping out at $6,500. Always consider the long-term affordability of any community in which you are interested.

Assisted living typically costs less than home health care or nursing home care. More than half of assisted living communities use a level of care pricing model with bundled services. One-quarter are all-inclusive and about 17 percent require a per service pay model.

Senior living pricing models, at best, can be complex and, at worst, downright confusing. Complicating the issue is that the pricing models and different nomenclature used at various communities may be so divergent as to make it difficult to truly comparison shop. Let's examine some of the more common pay models used in the industry.

ALL-INCLUSIVE PAY MODEL

As the name implies, "all-inclusive" communities cover everything: living quarters, food, housekeeping, laundry and linen, transportation, security, activities of daily living, recreational activities, and more. That means costs on a month to month basis are essentially the same, save for any value-added options the community might provide. Many seniors appreciate the predictability and communities appreciate the straightforward billing. If Medicare or insurance picks up some or all of the costs, reimbursements and payments are simpler to understand.

Changing needs can be handled without changing levels or pricing out individual services, reducing time and energy that need to be devoted to these alterations.

Please ask exactly what all-inclusive means because the term can vary from community to community. Some consider incontinence services or medication management to be added services and charge accordingly. Other extras may include spa or salon services, as well as gift shop or community store purchases.

Tuscan Gardens is an all-inclusive community for several reasons. Primarily, Tuscan Gardens was conceived to be the ultimate in concierge living. All the "extras" are part of the experience. We want our residents to move in and enjoy a life where every little detail is handled from what's for lunch to changing lightbulbs.

Advantage: Simple and predictable
Disadvantage: Usually the most expensive pay model

PER SERVICE (AL A CARTE) PAY MODEL

In a per-service scenario, residents typically pay a flat fee for rent or a room and board type plan. Any services above and beyond that are charged (either flat fees or hourly) if and when they are used. Hourly assistance fees may be charged per quarter hour or any portion of a quarter hour.

Realize, too, that community provision of services is likely to be of higher cost than one could obtain on the open market. Seniors who keep their own cars, use healthcare outside of the community (either with a good private health insurance plan or Veteran's Administration benefits) and cook for themselves pay significantly less than heavy users of services. The per service pay model is seldom seen in Memory Care situations.

Even those who anticipate using minimal services should benchmark pricing on more intensive services. Emergencies happen all the time and it's good to know what the costs might be in the event something unexpected happens. You might even want to start an emergency fund for just those types of occurrences.

Advantage: Ideal for healthy, active people
Disadvantage: Unpredictability

LEVEL OF CARE (A.K.A. TIERED PRICING) PAY MODEL

Some communities allow residents to choose a level of care (usually from three or four levels or tiers into which a variety of services are grouped) based on basic healthcare and daily needs. This continuum of care stretches from very basic (little to no care and, therefore, less expensive) to highly intensive (greatest care and most expensive), especially in those communities that handle memory care needs which become more severe over time. Often each level allows for a certain number of care hours per month.

Prospective residents are assessed upon moving in to ascertain their current care level needs. Re-assessments happen periodically to determine whether stepped up care is necessary.

By choosing levels of care, the pay structure reflects the care level. Therefore, you only pay for the care level you need when you need it. Moving from one level to another usually occurs in a seamless fashion with little worry or hassle. However, it may require moving from one wing to another in a community. If room and board represent a monthly fee of approximately $3,000, care related services may add another $1,000 to $1,500 to the total.

Some seniors take comfort in knowing the different pay levels up front and appreciate the fact that one community can be their permanent home regardless of when or how drastically their abilities diminish.

Advantage: Monthly bills reflect true needs
Disadvantage: Bill increases (often dramatically) as needs escalate.

ADDITIONAL FEES

Depending on the community, other fees may apply such as an application fee, entrance fee, community fee or moving in fee. These one-time fees may be equivalent to a full month's rent or even more. This type of charge may cover the cleaning or renovation of the living quarters or moving assistance. If these fees apply, the new resident may be required to cover this cost before move-in or in with their first month's payment.

The highest of these entry fees (possibly reaching several hundred thousand dollars) are typically associated with Continuing Care Retirement Communities (CCRCs).

Note: Entrance fees may be negotiable or waived entirely. Remember to ask!

Before we wrap up this section, here's a quick list of questions to ask when considering any community.

1. What's included in the all-inclusive pay model?

2. What's included in each level of care in a level of care model?

3. What's the breakdown of fees for each service in a per-service model?

4. What's not included and what's the process and fees for when services fall outside or exceed the pay model?

5. How do you track hours and care services?

6. What is your move-in/move-out procedure?

7. How often do you reassess a resident's care requirements?

8. What is the reassessment process?

9. Who is involved in the reassessment process, such as the resident, family members or outside medical experts?

10. Under what conditions would someone be asked to leave or be discharged?

11. What is the discharge process?

12. How much notice is given in a discharge situation?

13. What is your policy regarding theft?

14. What is your policy regarding renter's insurance?

15. What are your refund policies in the event a resident must move out or is asked to leave?

What you are seeking with this list of questions is price transparency. Senior living is one of the few industries left that doesn't have pervasive price transparency. However, as prospective residents perform greater online research, greater transparency is becoming available.

Price transparency in terms of all the fees and services will allow for educated consumers who can plan care costs and manage their expectations. Sticker shock should lessen when price transparency explains not only the number, but what goes into making up that figure.

For example, if pricing includes one hour of assistance per resident, per day, what constitutes assistance? Is it help with dressing or distributing medication? The effort level for each of those tasks is significantly different. Is housekeeping wiping off the countertops or scrubbing toilets? Is breakfast preparation yogurt and a banana or a hot cooked Denver omelet?

If all of this seems like too much to digest, consider getting professional help in terms of a guide or consultant. Amie Clark's book, *How to Choose Assisted Living Like a Pro*, offers an industry insider's viewpoint of the current senior living climate. Because the search for assisted living often occurs in crisis-mode, the pressure of locating a suitable care option in a short amount of time can lead to hasty choices. Amie's work with thousands of seniors, their families and healthcare professionals has led her to offer common sense advice and concrete choices.

DISCOUNTING

I'd like to close this section with a few thoughts on the practice of discounting. With the fierce competition for residents in the senior living industry, as well as the one-two punch the economy delivered in the earlier part of this century, discounting has been embraced by several communities to maintain census. In fact, according to research from the National Investment Center for Seniors Housing & Care, by the end of 2016, new assisted living residents were paying a rate that was an average of 10.7% lower than the original asking prices. That discount amounted to about 1.3 months' rent on an annualized basis.

As the recession placed a stranglehold on the real estate market, many seniors who normally would have moved into a senior living community stayed put because they simply couldn't sell their homes or couldn't sell their homes for the necessary price. Lowering rents or offering other financial incentives became a quick and easy way to boost occupancy and motivate prospective residents to sign on.

However, industry experts felt then, and continue to believe, that discounting creates doubt and sends the wrong message about the value of the product. Additionally, once one discount has been offered, further discounts will be expected. After all, if you cut your price once, why won't you do it again for other things?

Discounting, too, doesn't happen in a vacuum. Word travels and current residents who paid full price feel resentful that they weren't offered a freebie.

Discounting is a sensitive topic and one with which even the biggest players in the industry struggle. Senior living giant

Brookdale started 2016 with robust rate increases, banking in part on the improved economy and greater purchasing power by seniors. However, greater competition led Brookdale to take their foot off the gas so to speak with regard to pricing. Capital Senior Living employed discounts to offset a high level of move-outs, but did not attribute the move to a sense of stronger competition.

Some communities even have embraced "creative discounting," most notably Atlanta-based Isakson Living's Park Springs CCRC located in Stone Mountain, Georgia with its discount promotion modeled on one of Chick-fil-A's more famous practices.

When a new Chick-fil-A opens, the first 100 customers win a weekly free chicken sandwich meal for a year. Isakson put its own spin on that with its memory care expansion.

Park Springs has expanded to meet its aging resident base, adding 22 memory care units to its current 14. To ensure rapid occupancy of the new units, Isakson offered new memory care residents a "Price for Life" package. Price for Life guarantees that residents' monthly costs will not increase as they age, regardless of any additional care they may require.

While not a traditional discounting maneuver, Isakson hoped this lasting incentive helped the new units achieve faster stabilization. The promotion ended once the new units filled.

At its most basic, a discount used to close the deal is a "convincer." People who need to be convinced to buy anything, whether it's senior living or a steak dinner, tend to be harder to satisfy at the outset and as time passes.

Price can be a difficult conversation to have with regard to any large purchase. However, it tends to be a greater issue in terms of senior living. Very few people know anything about senior living until they are in a position to need it. With no frame of reference with regard to price vs. value, any dollar figure discussed early on monopolizes the issue when real feelings and emotions should dominate beginning conversations. Needs and budgets certainly must be considered, but quality of life, amenities, likes, and dislikes should be the initial concerns.

Beyond the fact that discounting can suggest that the product isn't worth the price, lowering prices can harm the community's bottom line. Quality care costs a certain amount of money, particularly in light of the fact that the acuity levels and, consequently, the care needs for many residents continue to increase. As one person put it, the healthiest day of your resident's life at your community is move-in day. Coupled with staffing issues, wage pressures, and capital improvements, the cost of doing business rises higher and rents are set to cover those situations.

Some communities only offer discounts on the lowest care levels, believing there is some room for sacrifice there. However, this sacrifice may be too dear if those discounted residents move on when their need level increases, preventing communities from recapturing lost profitability in the more expensive care tiers.

Tuscan Gardens isn't a budget choice, nor is it marketed as such. We stand by our product, knowing that the pricing is competitive, commensurate with the marketplace and the offered amenities. Benchmarking against other communities isn't the prime factor in our pricing, but rather understanding the true costs of providing each service.

Tuscan Gardens, like my other businesses, is metrics driven. We know what the exact costs are for every staff member (whether directly involved in resident care or not), taking into account their salary and benefits package, then adding overhead and building expenses. It becomes clear then, what one hour of that person's time really costs and how much we must charge for it.

Knowing the pricing metric is only half the battle, however. Next, it's crucial to know how much time is spent providing various services. If you are spit balling this, that's a big mistake. Chances are you are way off in terms of true time spent. That's because many people guesstimate the time they would spend doing something alone. In a senior living setting, you may be performing this task with an 80-year-old on your arm. That's why true tracking must take place.

True tracking also does its part to lessen associate burnout, a critical issue for senior living today. Associate burnout often occurs when residents are accessing more care than that which is allotted in their plan. A documentation tool will assist you and your staff to know exactly what you are providing and the time expended in doing so. In that way, residents are charged appropriately for the services they receive and associates aren't overworked in the process.

Pricing that reflects the true cost of service is fair to all parties and ensures the fiscal health of the senior living community.

If a community feels committed to offering incentives, consider non-financial motivators like assistance with moving in, unpacking boxes, and decorating.

HIGHLIGHTS

1. The sheer cost of senior living (particularly the higher levels of care) often takes prospective residents and their families by surprise, especially considering the difficulty in finding true pricing information online. Cost transparency will continue to be a hot topic in the industry.

2. The three main ways that individuals fund senior living are private pay, financial assistance, insurance, or some combination thereof.

3. When it comes to private financial sources, the primary residence represents most seniors' largest asset and the one commonly used for senior living in whole or in part.

4. Government subsidies may help in funding senior housing. However, assistance amounts are limited and seniors are restricted on the type of care received and facilities used for receiving that care.

5. Comparison shopping in senior living is made more difficult by various pricing models and different nomenclature.

6. Many communities have a wide range of additional or "hidden" fees. Make sure you understand everything before committing to a community.

CHAPTER 5

IN SEARCH OF AUTHENTICITY
CREATING A SENSE OF PLACE

*Traveling is the ruin of all happiness! There's no looking
at a building after seeing Italy.*
~ Fanny Burney

Conceptualizing Tuscan Gardens involved a holistic vision, based largely on my roots and firsthand experiences in that part of Italy. In my mind's eye, I recognized the Tuscan Gardens design aspect as I would recognize my own face in the mirror. From the architecture to the interior finishes to the operational functionality, I knew what I wanted to achieve. The challenge became effectively translating that vision to the professionals charged with moving from concept to creation.

MAINTAINING AUTHENTICITY

The key, of course, was achieving and sustaining authenticity. The experience I wanted to create had to be carried consistently and seamlessly from exterior to interior, with a single idea that tied the place together.

How often have you seen a beautiful building, perhaps a grand home, with charming French Provincial architecture that immediately transported you to the fields of Provence, only to enter the door and be assaulted by chrome and glass and hi-tech paraphernalia? That type of split personality undermines the design and fails to fulfill on the architectural promise.

On the other hand, I can remember, almost literally from the time I can remember anything – more or less, four or five years old – that no matter who came to our home and no matter how modest that environment was, particularly before Dad was able to get his bars as a second lieutenant and was still wearing the stripes of an Air Force sergeant, that the universal response was warmth and love. When anyone walked into the home, what they felt was the love, warmth, and the caring of an environment that embraced everyone within it.

That didn't change when I moved out of Mom and Dad's home and into my own life. As time went on, and as houses and family circumstances might have changed as I added on one, two and eventually a third child, the response was always the same. The circumstances might have been slightly more polished, but the feeling was nonetheless the same: *I feel love and warmth and caring in this home.*

The challenge was in creating an environment which emboldened the feeling and empowered the result.

In honoring a building's culture, historical context, and design, authenticity is achieved and the experiential promise is fulfilled when the core values of Tuscan Gardens are embraced.

AUTHENTICITY TUSCAN GARDENS STYLE

The design of the Tuscan Gardens emulates Tuscan architecture, stylistic features, and living patterns. Research indicates that Tuscan styling continues to be the most popular form of styling across the country, and particularly in Florida. Central to the design is an authentic over-sized Tuscan kitchen which is intended for community activity as much as for the preparation of food. Off the kitchen are two "Great Rooms," one to extend the dining and the other to extend the socializing. We'll discuss more about the components of a Tuscan Gardens community in "Chapter 6 Interior Spaces."

My initial focus in senior living was to develop communities on "A" quality sites, Tuscan theming notwithstanding, in upscale and mid-markets whose income, age cohort, and population reflect under-served markets. The foundation was an extended residential home and community with nothing that looked or felt institutional at any level – rather, a comfortable, classy, and upscale Ritz-Carlton.

We seek sites near hospitals and other medical services as well as proximity to shopping, restaurants, recreational and cultural activities, and major thoroughfares. As an added bonus, our locations in Florida afford us the opportunity to be near the Sunshine State's beautiful beaches.

The desired look for the end product was a Tuscan hillside village which just happened to have 180-plus private living quarters separated into three components – one each for supportive independent living, assisted living, and memory care as well as common areas and gardens for all three. The result is a senior living community that provides for a luxury residential environment with personalized concierge-quality care.

Bricks and mortar notwithstanding, the culture of Tuscan Gardens needed to inculcate, as best as I can describe, a general sense of what the Italians call "sprezzatura" or what the Americans water down as "charisma." Said differently, it is a comportment which reflects casual ease and grace above a foundation which is intentional – studied nonchalance.

Sprezzatura (Italian punctuation: [sprettsa'tura]) is the Italian word originating from Baldassare Castiglione's *The Book of Courtier*, where it is defined by the author as "a certain nonchalance, so as to conceal all art and make whatever one does or says appear to be without effort and almost without any thought about it." It is the ability of the courtier to display "an easy facility in accomplishing difficult actions which hides the conscious effort that went into them."

The best way I can describe it, in my terms, is that the culture maintains elegance and grace, charm, a sense of humor, easy going professionalism, playfulness, warmth, and compassion, as well as massive attention to both detail and to each and every individual.

The relevance of that cultural component needs to pervade every aspect of the architecture, design, styling, landscaping, programming, and human contacts. We had our work cut out for us.

At 11 years old, while I might not have known anything about the word *sprezzatura*, I knew what it meant in reality. Going to Hidden Lake, every summer, in Lindenwold, New Jersey, I got to be pretty good at ping pong. And, at 11 years old, I managed to compete with kids my age, as well as high schoolers all the way through senior year, as well as staff. I competed ferociously, but I never broke a sweat. In fact, somehow, deep down inside, it was not in my upbringing to ever demonstrate, imply or even suggest, that a game with any particular competitor, was worthy of competition. It was art at its finest – "an easy facility" hiding "the conscious effort" behind it.

In addition to *sprezzatura*, Tuscan Gardens' intention was to deliver what I call "residential intimacy," "family intimacy," or even "radical relational intimacy," despite the project's scale of anywhere from 96 to 235 units depending on the specific site. It is ultimately an architectural and design question as to how to do that the very best, but intention comes first.

Tuscan Gardens certainly pays homage to its Italian roots, while maintaining authenticity to its Florida home. Another community that does so, in a very different geographic locality is Berwick by the Sea in Campbell River, British Columbia. Looking somewhat like an oversized fisherman's lodge, Berwick by the Sea is a waterfront community on the east side of Vancouver Island. Its design honors the area's history as a fishing and logging community.

Another great example of authenticity is Carolina Bay at Autumn Hall. Located in Wilmington, NC and boasting Cape Fear Heritage architecture style, this CCRC sits on 17 acres, barely three miles from beautiful Wrightsville Beach. Called elegantly coastal, Carolina Bay's 330,000 square foot community fits within the larger master planned community of Autumn Hall.

To the extent that some readers of this book may indeed be envisioning creating their own senior living community that leverages *The Art of Living* as defined by them, at this point, it may be appropriate to share the common elements of the relational aspect. To my mind, they are:

- **Fusion Architecture**

- **Sense of the Aesthetic**

- **Integrative Value**

FUSION ARCHITECTURE

For those of you unfamiliar with fusion architecture, I would analogize to California Fusion food. "California Fusion" is a combination which consists of a certain amount of Asian, a certain amount of south of the border, and a certain amount of west coast new age organic.

In other words, my objective was not to be limited to strictly "Tuscan" architecture, but to create a fusion of that styling that allowed us to provide a look and feel which exemplified the quality and rhythm of the life I sought. Across the board, the fundamental narrative relates to the Italian lifestyle and the extraordinarily rich tapestry of Italy that underscores *The Art of Living*. That allowed us to lean heavily on Tuscany, Umbria, Rome, Piedmont, Puglia, Capri, and so forth.

Designwise, we wanted the style premised upon Tuscan architecture, but in the broader Mediterranean styling, not necessarily strictly Tuscan and certainly not necessarily farmhouse Tuscan; in other words, less of an overall Tuscan theme and more of a general Italian/Mediterranean theme.

The fusion styling I envisioned encompassed not only the initial 14th Century architecture and styling, but styling all of the way through the 16th Century. In addition, if you will remember from your history books, the Venetian style actually overlapped all of that. It encompassed a style which attempted to blend them all.

The "fused" end product turned out to be a general Italian Mediterranean style that allowed us to provide a local adaptation of each of those, provide creative expression, and not necessarily be narrowly typecast to just "Tuscan:" in other words, something authentic to our desired theming, but also observant of our Florida locale and respectful of the designers' innate creativity.

SENSE OF THE AESTHETIC

When I talk about the taste, styling, elegance, grace, and finesse, the end goal is a "sense of the aesthetic" — an appreciation for the quality of the contribution that history, art, finesse, and elegance offer us as human beings. As far as I'm concerned, our senior residents have certainly earned the right to live in that setting. They have fought the good fight their entire lives. Tuscan Gardens is the payoff.

The aesthetic is achieved not through massive amounts of dollars, but in judicious selection. There is a difference between spending a lot of money and having taste. Taste and class don't have to be expensive. What is expensive is cultivating the individual who appreciates taste, but that is a lifelong endeavor that we are not, thankfully, responsible for providing. Those with whom it resonates will be attracted to Tuscan Gardens and what it stands for. And better yet, we don't have to pay for them, we just need to make sure they know we exist.

One way in which this sense of the aesthetic is played out in a tangible fashion is through furniture, fixtures and equipment (FF&E), finishes, and artwork.

While most senior living facilities tend to be efficient, they rarely offer a luxurious residential environment of marble and deep wood grains. Tuscan Gardens is designed around that luxurious look with a warm feeling of comfort, intimacy, and a sense of scale familiar to seniors.

In bringing Tuscan Gardens to fruition, I focused on classy, elegant, and upscale finishes, such as deep woods, rich ceramics, terrazzo, actual china, and plush carpets. There is an adage that the difference between a competent architect or contractor and a luxury one is all about the finishes. And as to the finishes, both architecturally and from the standpoint of interior design, the objective was an exceptional high quality look and feel.

As for artwork, stock artwork is antithetical to *The Art of Living*. What could be more institutional than one of 10,000 poster prints run off at a local Kinko's and framed?

To me, *The Art of Living* demands original art, sculpture, and photography that represent real collectibles. Sourcing or creating these items would necessitate visiting higher quality and boutique art galleries, at least for the important pieces. Other items that would support a unique living environment would be creative adaptations of art objects, maps, portraits, and vases, as well as hand-made artifacts.

Considering the scale of artwork needed to decorate a 130,000 square foot community, not everything can be original. In this case, it's important to focus on the desired end result. That is, a sense of authenticity and aesthetic.

The average Tuscan Gardens community will require approximately 150 pieces of art; some of which will be major pieces that dictate our iconic imagery. Here's a look at the mix of artwork we achieve at every location.

First, three major pieces are installed in each location, all of them produced by a single artist. I've had this artist under contract for several years, but wanted him to walk the halls of the first Tuscan Gardens community, Tuscan Gardens of Venetia Bay, before he began work. It's important to me that he has a strong feel for the community and what it represents.

The first is a large-scale sculpture of an Etruscan horse in the front lobby. This iconic "Tuscan Gardens horse" becomes an image immediately identifiable with the Tuscan Gardens brand. This is in addition to other floor-standing sculpture in the interior and on the grounds.

The second, an original mural behind the front desk area, will transport the viewer to Tuscany and solidify the theming.

Third, as the inspiration for Tuscan Gardens, a formal portrait of my mother will hang in the Great Room. These three dominant pieces define the culture of Tuscan Gardens.

Another 25 or 30 pieces of fused liquid glass art have been sourced from an artist who just happens to be my sister, Joy. Joy has been a lifelong artistic explorer and through the years has found various outlets for expressing her creativity. Experimenting with diverse media and styles, Joy has found the perfect blend of color, form, and light with her glass pieces. While she began with small works, Joy has since pushed the envelope with ever-larger creations finally landing on large statement pieces as the perfect expression of her vision. The full-scale floor or tabletop pieces offer an artistic focal point to tie rooms together. Since Tuscan Gardens is a testament to my mother and her heritage, it's only fitting that Joy is represented in the halls as well.

Each Tuscan Gardens, while iconic and identifiable as its own unique setting, still resides within a local community. In an effort to reflect its surroundings, artwork from local artists also grace the walls. In each location, I've selected a dozen or so pieces from local artists working in a variety of media.

We've also contracted with a fabricator in Ravello, Italy, to produce original pottery for Tuscan Gardens. These pottery pieces have been selected specifically to bring a sense of authenticity to the halls.

Original photography, both recent and vintage shots, is a

contribution to the Tuscan Gardens' artistic puzzle. On our last visit to Italy, my family and I took some 800 photos. We hand-selected, in conjunction with Lisa Cini, some 30 or so to mat and frame for the walls of Tuscan Gardens at Venetia Bay. What makes these images so charming is that they are wonderful "real" scenes of modern Italy. Whether landscapes, people, buildings or even close-up shots of lemons or sunflowers, the images represent our own original contribution from myself, Janet, and our children.

Finally, a dozen black and white photos of my mother and her family at Il Palazzo Giordano, la Masseria or in Bari and its surroundings, comprise the vintage shots mentioned above. Each and every one tells a story. The old and new photography create a sense of family and place and personality.

As you can see, our approach to art is much more than "what can we use to fill a wall." Posters from the Internet can serve that purpose. Rather, we seek to surround residents with beauty and create the fusion of an experience. When they walk throughout the environment, we want them to enjoy a rich experience from the lush vegetation outdoors to the original artwork to the ambient music in the common areas.

The foregoing has been a snapshot of Tuscan Gardens' approach to design, but other communities should strive to be authentic to their own sense of the aesthetic.

For some, that's sourcing vintage pieces that reflect the younger days of their average resident. While some designers can't spend hours haunting second-hand shops or antique stores, several manufacturers offer reproductions made in vintage style but with today's sturdier materials.

Other communities that embrace sustainability seek to re-use salvaged materials. These materials don't necessarily need to relive their original function. Rather, uniquely repurposing an old door as a unique glass-topped coffee table allows for creativity and visual interest.

Using recycled or vintage pieces differentiates a community, pays homage to history and allows residents to relive their salad days. Of course, care must be taken with reclaimed or older items to ensure their safe "re-use." It can be money or time intensive to refurbish these unusual items, so those things should be considered. When in doubt, leveraging an item as artwork or an architectural item rather than a functional piece of furniture can be a better choice.

In any case, planning is the key word whenever non-traditional items are used. Understand whether refurbishing needs to take place and the "effort level" required. Do you need a certified contractor or tradesman, or perhaps just a general handyman? What is the timeline necessary for achieving the refurbishment? The best-case scenario is sourcing items from professionals who have or can refurbish the items in a one stop shop.

No matter what, only work with businesses or individuals that understand the unique requirements of a senior living setting. It helps if they have familiarity with the code limitations inherent in senior living, as well as the needs of seniors when it comes to their greater risk for falls, sensitive skin and potential visual impairment.

On a final note before transitioning to a discussion about basic functionality, I'd like to say a few words about signage, since some people think signage serves as its own "artwork."

Signage, in general, creates an institutional feel. A residence does not have a sign that says "Office," "Therapy," "Kitchen," "Media Room," and so forth. Institutions do; homes do not. And, a senior living community is the residents' home. Therefore, I recommend using only signage absolutely required by law. The exception to this is signage that might be appropriate for Memory Care residents to enhance their ability to live as autonomously as possible. I'll discuss this in those appropriate chapters.

The exception to this when it comes to Tuscan Gardens comes from two specific signs which are intended to be prominent and visible in every Tuscan Gardens Community. These signs override my previous mandate on signs because they embody everything that Tuscan Gardens is and everything it stands for.
The first placed outside the main front entrance to the community reads: *Parva Sed Apta Nobis*. The second in the back courtyard placed in or around the community's major water feature: *Sempre Famiglia*.

FUNCTIONALITY

The look and feel of Tuscan Gardens, or any senior living community, notwithstanding, its functional design must be appropriate for seniors, meaning any exterior or interior concepts must meet a senior's desire to live independently and safely. Ideally, any senior's living arrangement should embrace structural elements and assistive technology that prevent accidents and lead to an enhanced quality of life.

One of the benefits of living in a senior community is that the living areas have already been designed or adapted for older individuals. Studies show that most older people live in homes that are more than 20 years old. That means that seniors are faced with three options:

- Do nothing as their homes become harder to live in and maintain

- Invest in retrofitting projects that may cost time, money, and stress

- Move into "turnkey" type senior living communities that have all the necessary design elements

With regard to the second option, the national Centers for Disease Control and Prevention show that home modifications and repairs may prevent 30% to 50% of all home accidents such as tripping and falling. In fact two-thirds of the falls suffered by seniors happen at home. However, the costs may be prohibitive or the negative design elements impossible to overcome. All remodeling or retrofitted adjustments must comply with one or more of the following: the Fair Housing Amendments Act of 1988, the Americans with Disabilities Act accessibility guidelines, American National Standards Institute regulations for accessibility, and any state or local building codes.

One of the concerns many older homeowners have when it comes to retrofitting their homes is the potential resale value of a property that has been modified. Features that can be made quickly to enhance the adaptability of a home (and possibly be quickly reversed without a complete redesign to the structure) tend to be the most desirable.

According to the Rehabilitation Engineering and Assistive Technology Society of North America (RESNA), one key element that should be observed when it comes to appropriate design for seniors is improved accessibility.

Improved accessibility may be achieved through wider doorways that allow wheelchairs or walkers to pass through unimpeded. Also included are lower sinks, countertop heights, and light switches for people permanently in wheelchairs, as well as higher electrical outlets.

According to a study by AARP, the main reasons for not undertaking home modifications for senior living included the inability to make the required changes on their home and inability to afford the required changes.

One advantage senior living communities have over the "do nothing" or retrofitting options is that many communities already observe universal design principles. The term "universal design," also called "inclusive design," was coined by architect Ronald L. Mace to describe a building design that creates an end product that is inherently accessible and usable to the greatest extent possible by all people, regardless of age, ability or status in life.

In short, universal design embraces barrier-free concepts without sacrificing aesthetics. Materials used in universal design tend to be sturdy and reliable. Functionality requires minimal effort and understanding of the mechanics involved.

EXTERIOR AND COMMON AREA ELEMENTS

- Elevators or chair lifts

- Handrails on both sides of staircases that are wide enough to allow them to be grasped securely

- Wider doorways

- Curb cuts and sidewalk ramps

- Wheelchair ramps with proper ramp width and slope per local and state cost. Under the Uniform Building Code, a wheelchair ramp must have a minimum length of 8 feet for a rise of 12 inches (1:8), although a length of 12 feet per 12-inch rise is recommended for safety (1:12). So, for example, if your front steps rise 16 inches, your ramp would have to be at least 10.7 feet long to comply with the Code, with a length of 16 feet recommended. Minimum width is 3 feet, and a 34-

38-inch high railing is required unless the slope is less steep than 1:15.

• Well-lit hallways and common areas

My goal with Tuscan Gardens has been to incorporate the authentic design covered in the beginning of this chapter without ever losing sight of the functionality for seniors. Done well and in concert, you get the best of both worlds.

HIGHLIGHTS

1. Authenticity is achieved when a building's culture, historical context, and design are honored and aligned.

2. Fusion architecture allows the marriage between creative theming and geographic locale while still observing the necessary requirements for a senior living environment. That being said, design cannot eclipse functionality, particularly when it comes to seniors.

3. The sense of the aesthetic in a senior living community can easily be played out in a tangible fashion through furniture, fixtures and equipment (FF&E), finishes, and artwork.

4. Avoid "filling a wall" when you can solidify the community experience through carefully selected artwork.

5. Signage reinforces an institutional feel and should be used only when necessary or mandated by law.

6. Retrofitting an existing home may not be appropriate for many seniors and, therefore, a senior living community could be the best option.

CHAPTER 6

INTERIOR SPACES

All architecture is shelter, all great architecture is the
design of space that contains, cuddles, exalts,
or stimulates the persons in that space.
~ Philip Johnson

When I began conceptualizing Tuscan Gardens in 2010, it made a great deal of sense to visit current communities. In the same way a couple might tour model homes to see not only what's available on the market, but to crystallize their own preferences, I wanted to do my own market research.

In addition, I turned to invaluable publications such as *Building Type Basics for Senior Living* by Bradford Perkins and J. David Hoglund. This comprehensive volume covers all aspects of the design of senior living communities, including examples of completed projects, information on the latest developments in senior living design, content on sustainable design, renovation and reinvention, international opportunities, operations, and project financing.

In doing so, I was struck by what I considered a counterintuitive sense of scale. At most communities I toured, the private living suites seemed minuscule and the common areas literally cavernous. To my way of thinking, this works against the desired intimacy we wanted to create among seniors who can be predisposed at the outset to loneliness and isolation (see discussion of this in "Chapter 3: The Case For Community").

A SENSE OF SCALE

Current accepted practice suggests that the overall size

of a senior living community should range between 50% to 100% of the square footage of the private living suites. To me those formulas are way off. The architectural plan for Tuscan Gardens provides for common areas of approximately 30% of the total square footage allocated to the private living suites and no more than 10% to "back of house" infrastructural support.

I marketed sales and fulfillment events across the country for over 20 years. These events ranged from small meetings of 20 or 30 individuals to large conferences of 10,000 people. No matter what the size, I inevitably cut the allocated space recommendations in half (but always in observance of fire codes and occupancy levels, of course).

In my experience, the quality of the experience was far greater when putting 3,000 people into hotel sleeping rooms of appropriate size, but common areas of half the size. Was there less common area? Of course. Was there greater enjoyment and quality of experience? Absolutely.

Intimacy is created when space supports people being together, not apart. The opportunity to be apart is easy enough – when you've had enough time socializing, simply go to your otherwise spacious private suite. In the case of my example, retreat to your own hotel room.

The same holds true in all of the communities I had seen – at least when I was envisioning Tuscan Gardens. They appear to suffer from two primary architectural defects in terms of size: first, the private living suites are too small; and second, the common areas are too large.

Frankly, it's not even clear to me what the architect or operator is going for by creating massive scale. These are seniors. It requires them to ambulate more, slows down passage to go from one place to another and increases the separation between individuals.

From a cost efficiency standpoint, it also costs more to construct and maintain. There is no good reason why private living suites have to be as small as I have seen and common areas as large as I have seen.

I saw an assisted living facility recently which was otherwise beautifully designed, except that the total square footage was composed of 100% allocated to private living suites and 120% allocated to common areas and back of house infrastructure.

Without even knowing what those percentages were, I made the comment to the architect that the design was beautiful except that the size of the common areas needed to be cut in half.

Not everyone agrees with this assessment. One community, Overture Plan, the 2016 Senior Housing News Design Award winner for best independent living, boasts very ample communal space – some 16,000 square feet. Located about a 30-minute drive from Dallas, the community's hip and young vibe has made it a winner with seniors 55 and older.

CEILINGS, WINDOWS, AND WALLS

While the common areas should be much more intimate than the typical senior living community, high ceilings and natural light contribute to a greater sense of size. How often have you been in a light airy room with high ceilings and plenty of sunlight that seemed quite spacious only to be told that the dimensions are much smaller than you imagine? Ample windows for natural light and high ceilings to reflect that opportunity provide a sense of verticality, both externally and internally.

Contributing to this sense of lightness and airiness are minimal barriers from room to room. While in the common areas walls can't be eliminated, they can be minimized. There is a clear function for a wall which provides both support and a separation of functions.

However, walls are over-rated when they separate functions that could otherwise be contiguous with an interior design feature separating the space, rather than a wall.

For example, a wall obviously has to separate a private suite from the common area off of which the private suite is based – what I'm calling a "pod" and which is discussed below. That's an obvious use for a wall. A wall also has to be used to separate the space for specific activities. Tuscan Gardens provides what we call "Il Cinema Paradiso," a cinema where residents can watch a movie separated from the noise, conversation or distraction of what's happening in the Great Rooms. That's an appropriate use for a wall.

However, Great Rooms should not be divided from each other, from the front entrance or from the flow of traffic. Open areas and common areas should encourage a free flow of traffic with dividers only when functional reasons dictate. In these cases, dividers should be relegated to things like waist-high separators (half walls) that don't impede vision or artistic elements which simply navigate the flow of traffic in a particular direction, but don't otherwise impede the traffic.

When full walls are called for, it's desirable to approach the idea with creativity and "double duty" in mind. I visited one senior living community that makes use of a "living wall" of herbs. Located near the dining area, the herb wall is a charming reminder of the fresh and wholesome food on order, artfully flavored with fresh offerings from the wall. Nothing is more delightful than seeing the executive chef in chef whites and toque come around the corner to snip the basil and rosemary needed for that evening's meal.

In all circumstances, the emphasis should be on those natural dividers representing aesthetic contributions and/or horticultural contributions, not physical barriers. If they do their job in the aesthetic and horticultural component, they will fulfill the physical components.

INTEGRATING COMMON AREAS AND PRIVATE SPACES

Having covered the basic conceptual layout of common areas and private living suites, let's discuss how the two areas integrate. Ideally, connecting hallways should be minimized, if not eliminated altogether.

Does anybody like a hallway? While they are functional, are they not also scary? It absolutely boggles my mind that assisted living communities, like hotels, have long hallways with doors on either side for individuals to peel off. It is almost as bad as Kafka's *The Castle*. It is a never-ending nightmare of a self-elongating hallway that never has an end.

Naturally, from an architectural or a functional standpoint, some hallways are required, certainly in back of house. However, creative design can allow for any number of other alternative interior designs which will provide the functionality that a hallway has in the front of the house while at the same time eliminating the look and feel of a hallway.

Tuscan Gardens' solution for minimizing hallways is to introduce small – not large – pods for the private suite area.

Consider, if you will, six private living suites feeding off one central "pod" in a sort of spoke and hub concept. The common pod might be no more than 5% to 10% of the total square footage of the private living suites, but would provide a common sitting or gathering area. Hence, imagine a pod of eight rooms in three sections with a common "living space." Three sections time eight rooms times three floors equal 72 rooms, but radical intimacy is not lost.

My Mother's home, which we bought for her when Dad passed away, was perfect for a senior. It had no hallways. It simply had rooms off of the two primary common areas, which consisted of the dining area (kitchen) and the socialization area (living room). All three private living suites and bathrooms, as well as the laundry room and garage, stemmed off of that common area.

To the extent that the primary common areas of Tuscan Gardens involve the two "Great Rooms" – the "dining area" and the "socialization area" – virtually all other functional rooms could stem off of those without the crutch of a hallway.

SOCIALIZING AND DINING

Socialization areas must make use of some larger seating areas, but many more nooks and crannies where individuals can interact on a more intimate and personal basis.

Rather than walls, natural dividers like potted palms or sculpture allow for private, although not disconnected, contact. In touring this Great Room, you might take note of two residents having a conversation without being able to hear what they're saying.

With respect to the dining area, the goal was to create opportunities for socialization and intimacy on a family dining level. Therefore, while some two-tops and four-tops may be appropriate, the majority of tables would be of the larger eight- and ten-top varieties. This psychology also supports the smaller scale common areas. Based on this, the dining room square footage is less than typically accounted for, but community interaction is enhanced.

A study by the University of Toronto supports this approach. The study concluded that serving family style (large portions where people "pass their plate") and a homelike dining environment optimize energy intake for residents at high risk for malnutrition, particularly those with low body mass indices and cognitive impairment.

A study by Wageningen University shows an increase in quality of life, physical performance, and body weight between groups of residents based on the dining style, shown in the following graph. Family-style dining vs. pre-plated meals boosted those factors and led to improved dining ambiance as well.

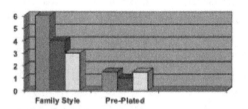

Policies of open seating at all mealtimes enhance socialization, irrespective of the residents' natural tendency to focus in earnest on their conversation. Sitting with different people allows for new friendships. *"Anytime Socialization"* is encouraged: it reduces "room service" meals, which leads to better service in the dining room.

The dining room and private living suites shouldn't be the only choices for enjoying a meal or snack. Outside patios, lounges or libraries equipped with snack tables or side tables let residents eat wherever they please.

Further extended mealtimes make any community more homelike. Nobody really cares if you want eggs and bacon at 3 p.m. in your own home, do they? Allowing residents to eat whenever, wherever and whatever they want makes a community feel like home and allows residents to linger over meals (increasing nutrient intake and possibly eliminating the need for snacks or costly supplements).

This type of anytime dining reinforces the current "small plates" trend, too. Small plates allow diners to try a little bit of several dishes rather than one large plate of a single item. Several small plates are an ideal way to share and socialize as well.

The small plate movement has taken hold everywhere — on university campuses, in hospital cafeterias and now in senior living. Driven by the fact that mealtimes are less clear cut than they used to be and people tend to graze throughout the day, small plates fill the bill and the stomach – particularly for senior residents.

Small plates also encourage trying new things. One small appetizer portion of an exotic or foreign dish (or an unusual fusion of two seemingly divergent cuisines) seems safer than committing to a full plate of an unknown entrée.

Please note, implementing the small plate trend may require planning in advance. Larger tables may be needed to handle more plates. Special serving utensils for sharing could also be required. Plus, servers shouldn't be shy about recommending groupings of small plates that offer interesting taste mixes.

If 24/7 "anytime" dining is impossible, a 7 a.m. to 7 p.m. schedule might be doable. Cold foods like ready-made sandwiches, fruit plates or "homemade" frozen dinners for reheating in their private living suites can help you extend dining hours. This type of "hospitality" meal is also a benefit when residents would like to entertain in their private living quarters.

Remember, nowhere is the concierge trend in senior living more evident than in dining. Ensuring that you have the newest tastes and trends, presented attractively and served in gracious surroundings sends the message that *The Art of Living* happens on your premises.

While the dining room and socialization areas are the two primary Great Rooms, they are by no means the only ones. The main socialization areas can and should flow into other natural settings.

Tuscan Gardens, for example, has an area dedicated to music, including a grand piano, as well as other instruments. This area provides a place for residents to congregate when there is a chamber ensemble recital or some type of musical event. As you might have guessed, the area is more formal, because of the nature of it.

Picture, for example, an opera singer doing a recital accompanied by a three or four instrument chamber ensemble, a simple pianist coming in for a recital of a particular type of music, a guitar player coming in as a singer/songwriter, a harpist performing or even a local grade, middle, or high school and/or its orchestra.

Ambient music is also played throughout the community,

using a service provider like Sonos or Mood Media. As a company, Mood Media combines sight, sound, scent, social mobile technology, and systems solutions to create greater emotional connections between brands and customers.

Sonos is a wireless Sound System that sets up quickly and makes listening easy. By using a free app, Sonos can connect directly to the Wi-Fi network and send different songs to different rooms at the same time. Alternatively, one big favorite may be enjoyed in perfect sync all through the common areas. Sonos plays all the most popular music services, internet radio, audiobooks, podcasts, music downloads – it can even be set up to play a vinyl collection.

This type of social area should be multi-functional enough to accommodate not only these varied musical interludes, but also other recreational or programmatic events.

Other areas incorporated into Tuscan Gardens that can be considered for other communities:

- The aforementioned media room or cinema that seats 12 to 18 at any particular time to allow for screening movies on an ongoing basis. Tuscan Gardens' media room replicates a full cinema with a large theater-quality style screen and comfortable dining appropriate for residents without design concerns, lifted areas, steps or the like.

- Activities rooms as appropriate, although less than would be conventionally prescribed. Activities are intentionally centered on no more than two rooms to ensure maximum activity at any particular time in those two areas.

- Occupational therapy and physical fitness rooms. Both functions matter, but there is no reason to separate the two. These activities can be done simultaneously and just simply handled logistically.

- Beauty and hair styling salon with opportunities for facials, manicures, and more.

- A fully technologically enabled medical office that allows us to provide for telemedicine and a connection with each resident's doctor without the need to transport the residents from place to place. Video conferencing capability between the individual resident on our side and the doctor on the other side provides, from a programmatic standpoint, an in-person visitation process for a doctor who represents a medical group that services the community. However, over and above that, we incorporate a telemedicine technology to allow our residents to be supported by whomever they choose on the medical side.

• Lastly, a small dedicated room serves as an inter-denominational chapel, accommodating approximately 12 individuals.

Remember, too, that the socialization areas, while not primarily eating areas, can be leveraged for special dining opportunities. Tuscan Gardens offers high tea in the Great Room, not the dining area. Any senior living community would do well to factor in multiple opportunities and uses for common area space.

TRANSFORMING KITCHENS TO "FRONT OF THE HOUSE" FOCAL POINTS

While not technically a common area, the kitchen provides a unique opportunity to transform what has traditionally been a "back of the house" space to a "front of the house" on-stage area. And, as you might imagine, the kitchen in a community called Tuscan Gardens is something even more iconic, both from an architectural as well as from a programmatic standpoint. It is as much a central focal point of socialization as the food itself.

The Tuscan Kitchen at Tuscan Gardens reflects the wonderful chemistry of a Tuscan chef, surrounded by the tools of his trade, producing incredibly fresh organic food on a real time basis in front of residents and guests. All of those elements are central branding elements of Tuscan Gardens.

On the IL and AL sides, the Tuscan Kitchen is a major component of the area that abuts the social Great Room and the dining Great Room. In fact, it is somewhat of a functional divider in the sense that, on one side, you have the social area and on the other side you have the dining area. It is intended to be visible not only from both of those areas, but it's also intended to be visible from the front door.

While the common areas in general have been kept on the more modest or "intimate" size, the Tuscan Kitchen occupies a greater than typical space to allow multiple functions. It is not only an area where food is prepared, but also in which cooking classes and demonstrations occur, the community comes in for entertainment and lessons, and residents and nonresidents are incorporated into an outreach program that produces a valuable contribution to the community.

Whereas staff member makeup is covered much more comprehensively in "Chapter 13: Creating Community, Conversation & Culture," from a programmatic standpoint, it is appropriate to discuss the Culinary Manager & Executive Chef here. Beyond technical expertise, culinary talent should have gregarious personalities and that little bit of showmanship that allows them to communicate compassionately, professionally, enthusiastically, and in an entertaining way to the residents. Think about any of the cast of characters shown on The Food Network on any given day. In Disney nomenclature, consider the Executive Chef and Assistant Chef to be "cast members" who play a role as much as perform a function.

At Tuscan Gardens, what is really relevant to us is having individuals working the food program who are real "foodies" with a knowledge of and a passion for food. We seek real chefs who have created a body of work that may include original restaurant selections and gourmet dishes. Our current Culinary Director in Venice is a former restaurateur who worked the kitchen and back of the house while his wife handled the front. As such, he is well acquainted with crafting authentic original recipes from fresh ingredients and customizing them to individual diner's tastes as necessary. This individual does not create by "opening cans" nor does he follow some "feeding seniors" handbook. Not only is he incredibly passionate about providing five-star service, he truly cares that the residents love the food.

Our Culinary Manager & Executive Chef follows a similar path of not only being a restaurateur as well as an executive chef with substantial experience in senior living communities, but also a food aficionado. On his interview with Tuscan Gardens, he not only laid out original recipes he had created... and prepared... but he also came with luscious photography of the very dishes he had created from original and authentic ingredients. To hear him speak is to be very clear that this is a person who loves what he does and loves food.

It was incredibly important to the Tuscan Gardens culture that the centerpiece of our community was a Tuscan Kitchen and the heartbeat of our zeitgeist was signature dining.

As an all-inclusive community, Tuscan Gardens offers anytime dining. Residents can wander in at any time and see the chefs placing good, fresh food in the exposed bread oven, including pastries, flatbreads, and pizzas. Whenever possible, the food is made out in front, right under the watchful eye of the resident who ordered it.

In designing a kitchen such as the one described, it must be organized to allow the Executive Chefs to deliver at every level. The dynamic nature of dining trends and desires requires a flexible environment that allows the experience to evolve over time. Fixtures may include a gas stove, a bread/pizza oven, and exposed racks for hanging pots and pans. Architecturally, the space should incorporate islands or live cooking stations for demonstration and sampling of foods and allow for the natural exposure of all of the cooking aromas and fragrances to make sure that the residents inhale the scents of basil, fresh bread, tomatoes, zucchini, and more.

Lastly, the kitchen should be organized to allow customization of meals. Customization, remains a solidly popular way to order and enjoy meals. Customization allows diners to order food in a very specific way to make it personal. The experience is heightened if the food is fresh and visible right in front of you.

Customization works best when it springboards off some sort of "platform," be it pizza crust, pita pocket, rice bowl or salad. The toppings and add-ons allow diners to create something uniquely their own.

As it was originally conceptualized, Tuscan Gardens included only IL and AL components. In that initial architectural layout, the Tuscan Kitchen could be seen obliquely from the front door, but actually faced the back door.

Including Memory Care flipped not only our thinking, but the placement of the Tuscan Kitchen itself. Now, the Tuscan Kitchen actually faces the front door reflecting the fact that its back wall is shared with an institutional kitchen that supports not only the front

Assisted Living, but also the back Memory Care which cannot – and probably should not – for obvious reasons, have an exposed kitchen.

A positive by-product of this altered layout is that it also allows the opportunity to conjoin the Assisted Living and Memory Care with one centralized kitchen supporting both services, but with an exposed Tuscan Kitchen on the front and a dining environment for Memory Care consistent with the theme of Tuscan Gardens, though not otherwise exposed to the Tuscan Kitchen. That same area would also support back of house functions.

DINING TECHNOLOGY

The discussion of the kitchen and eating venues wouldn't be complete without mention of technology that is currently driving dining. Many restaurants, be they in the community, hospitals or senior living communities, encourage online and mobile ordering and tablets for menus and payments. Digital menu boards offer graphics, animated images, videos, and interactivity with regard to loyalty programs or nutrition information.

Technology in general is used to increase speed of service. Beyond the convenience factor, online ordering ensures precise ordering and improves efficiencies and throughput.

All this being said, any senior living community must decide the role that technology will play in its operations, particularly its dining operations. While Tuscan Gardens would be considered progressive when it comes to technology, the dining venue may be one place where we stick to old school. If, as posited in the above paragraph, technology is about making things go faster, we want people to linger over meals. For some, it's the highlight of their day and having a second glass of wine allows them to savor the moment.

For us, it's about being authentic to our premise, *The Art of Living*; other communities will make decisions based on their unique needs and markets.

PRIVATE LIVING SUITES

As has already been mentioned, traditional senior living communities tended to give short shrift to the apartments when it comes to space allocation – a situation, thankfully, which is changing rapidly. My viewpoint is that's backward. At Tuscan Gardens, we refer to bedrooms as "private living suites" for a number of reasons. First, the private living suites come in various sizes and configurations and, as a result, the concept is to refer to them as a living area as opposed to a sleeping area. Second, they are "private" living suites as opposed to "living suites" because it is intended that the entire building represents their living area as a residence.

Capitalizing on the "pod" psychology cited above, Tuscan Gardens offers a centralized pod of six to eight private living suites feeding off a small hub. Each is extremely generous in size as compared to traditional senior living community living spaces and designed to allow exterior walls to face gardens or finely landscaped areas. Some ground floor units have floor to ceiling windows (with no external door), upper floor units have much more than a simple window. Both plans allow maximum access to the landscaping around the building.

Private living suites offer ample living areas (not just a bedroom) and an upscale, multi-functional kitchenette. For example, the private living suites that we are providing for the IL units range from 550 square feet to 1100 square feet; AL units range from 500 square feet to 975 square feet; and in Memory Care from 300 square feet to 450 square feet. Those are extremely generous and substantial in senior living.

The generous spaces for the private side of senior living coupled with the scaled back common areas provide comfortable and luxurious private living and far greater intimacy and social contact in public areas.

Despite the beautiful aesthetics of any senior suite, the functionality must be designed and executed for an older resident. Some things to consider on a room by room basis include:

Within the kitchen:

- "Pull-style" cabinet handles

- Sliding and lazy Susan type revolving shelves

- Easy to use and clearly marked appliance controls

- Easy open oven and refrigerator doors

- Conveniently located appliances and utensils

- Induction style cooktop that offers a cool cooking surface for safety

- Comfortable (wheelchair) counter height and depth

- Slightly raised (approximately 1/4 inch) front of the refrigerator that will allow the door to close by itself

- Color contrast dishware with steep sides to help with seniors who have visual or dexterity problems

Within the bathroom:

- Roll-in shower stalls and/or walk-in tubs with a door, built-in seating and non-skid strips

- Elevated toilet seats

- Grab bars located by the tub/shower and toilet

- Handheld flexible shower heads

- Lever-operated faucets for easy turn on/off

- Well-regulated water temperature (water heater set at 120 degrees Fahrenheit) to prevent scalding or burning

- Ample room to allow a caregiver to provide assistance to a resident

Within the bedroom:

- Convenient closets and ample storage with proper shelf height and modular shelf systems to maximize storage space

- Emergency lighting

General:

• Easy to open, close, and lock windows and doors.

• Lower door peepholes for security

• Flush thresholds with no step up/step down.

• Non-slip/non-skid flooring (no throw rugs) with any deviations (steps or inclines) properly marked

• Easy to reach and operate light switches and electrical outlets (properly grounded)

• Whole house wiring to allow intercom, smoke detectors, emergency alarms, night lighting

• Programmable phones with one-digit speed dial for emergency or often dialed numbers

• Wide stairs that accommodate the whole foot

• Sufficient lighting for each room's needs and functions, possibly using track lighting with halogen lamps and dimmer switches in most rooms

• Proper ventilation in all rooms with good air circulation

• No chairs on furniture on casters or wheels

• Sturdy risers under other furniture items to raise them

• No decorative "clutter items" on floors such as baskets, plants or small ottomans

MEMORY CARE LIVING QUARTERS

Memory Care living quarters should achieve the highest level of normalcy possible. The suggestions listed below are designed specifically for Memory Care, but can also be incorporated in any care level from IL to AL. The goal is to create an environment that isn't unduly restrictive, but very safe to function in. Room design should be customized to the level of support the resident requires and necessary changes due to the increased level of care normalized to the greatest extent possible.

Because white rooms are difficult for individuals with dementia to navigate (frequently they appear circular), using colored paint on walls provides contrast. In fact, using two or more coordinating colors to paint accent walls allows for colorful focal points. However, medium shades are best. Dark and bright shades of any color can be hard for dementia patients to perceive and process. Red is an active color and painting a door red may not only make it easier to distinguish from the wall, it can encourage a person to leave their room more frequently.

On the other hand, if you want to discourage wandering, paint exit doors the same color as the walls to divert attention from leaving. Wandering can be defined as either random or goal driven. Increasing engagement helps prevent both types. Ask for help with activities or provide a box filled with desirable activities or objects. Pre-printed notes that explain you will be back soon (even if you have only gone into the next room) help discourage wandering in patients who have forgotten that you are nearby.

Exit-seeking is a critical issue among the dementia community with six out of 10 people exhibiting wandering behaviors, which can increase anxiety, hostility toward others, fatigue, and elopement.

Due to the serious nature of exit-seeking, many communities are incorporating designs into their environments that reduce the tendency to wander. Wandering or the desire to wander typically occurs when family members or friends leave after a visit. The moment of departure can cause agitation and a desire to "go home too" on the part of the resident.

That's why Watercrest Senior Living's Market Street Memory Care Residences are designed with a central market plaza. The plazas, which look very much a like a town square, display storefronts and seating areas, making them an ideal place for visits. To exit from this pleasant area, visitors move through a type of holding area before hitting a keypad to reach the main reception area. Should a resident follow, the holding area is designed to look like a post office with a newsstand. The resident can then be distracted by the magazines and other items.

Another company, Creative Art Co., has begun printing large scale "door disguisers" to assist with preventing wandering. These large adhesive murals transform exit doors into "bookcases" or "china cabinets."

Additional suggestions, many of which come from my good friend and award-winning memory care program developer, Joshua Freitas, include:

- Keeping coats, umbrellas and boots out of sight which can help discourage wandering. Ask visitors to leave coats or jackets in a cloak room, otherwise the resident may become agitated and want to go "home" with their loved one.

- Furniture selection and arrangement should be minimal and simplistic. Avoid using small area rugs to decrease the likelihood of slips, trips, and falls. If that's impossible, place adhesives on the back to firmly affix them in place.

- Keep the environment scrupulously clean and reduce clutter. Organize belongings and remove extraneous items. Use mirrors in the living environment judiciously (if at all) to reduce distraction and spatial confusion. Ensure that any houseplants are non-toxic.

- The subject of clutter also extends to small objects that may be in use in a suite. Because visual impairment affects 75% of people over age 65 (not just those with dementia), small items should be carefully monitored. Paperclips, push pins and coins can easily be mistaken for edibles like candy or nuts. Eliminate or minimize these items or replace them with larger, lower risk items.

- Enhance visibility and reduce the chance of falls by increasing the amount of light in the living quarters. However, keep in mind the amount of artificial light. Make use of large windows to show natural light during the day and indicate the changing time as sunset approaches. Place digital (not analog) clocks in the living area to also reinforce time of day.

- Natural light creates awareness of time of day to dementia patients. After dark, make liberal use of nightlights in bedrooms, bathrooms, and hallways.

- In the kitchen, monitor the small appliances and household objects in use. Coffee makers and toaster ovens (if used) need automatic shutoff functionality. Sharp knives should be out of reach, but not locked away. Encountering locked doors and drawers gives dementia patients a feeling of being limited or restricted and can lead to negative behaviors such as exit seeking. That's why dangerous items (if they need to be in the living quarters at all) should be placed out of reach and out of sight.

- Red serving ware has been shown to increase appetite in dementia patients. Red dishes also provide a clear contrast between food and plate, making the meal easier to see.

- It bears noting that keeping safe objects around can be therapeutic for dementia patients. Repetitive behaviors arising from boredom and obsessive tendencies are indicative of Alzheimer's disease. Organizing objects can ameliorate obsessive, negative behaviors like hoarding or stealing. Set aside a drawer for rummaging or organizing space. If a person consistently steals or hoards, knowing they can put items in their special drawer provides comfort, stability and calm, but allows caregivers to know where to find missing items.

- Keeping the kitchen filled with thick-handled utensils and plate guards can make eating easier. Storing items where a person expects to find them can enhance their ability to live independently. Bread in a breadbox and toothbrushes in toothbrush holders assist in day to day functioning. Labels and signs help with the identification, organization, and use of items. Any "safe" item that is used frequently should not be hidden or inaccessible, but kept out in the open.

- Medications shouldn't be left on the kitchen counters, tables or even in bathroom medicine cabinets to prevent self-medication or over-medication. Administer any prescriptions under supervision. Both medicines and dangerous cleaning chemicals should be stored away. In fact, multipurpose cleaning products can be replaced with a safe spray bottle of vinegar solution.

• Bathroom doors should be left open to provide a visual cue about the purpose of that room. If that is impossible, place a photograph of a toilet on the bathroom door. In general, photographs do a great job of identifying the nature of places and things in the living quarters. Photos of clothes on closet doors and food on the front of the refrigerator are also good ideas.

• Like living rooms, all white bathrooms are undesirable. Use color on the walls and select a contrasting colored toilet seat to direct attention and allow the resident to find the toilet easily.

• Color also applies to bed linens. Rather than white bedding, use different colors for sheets, blankets and pillowcases to help distinguish each type of item from the others. Arrows on the interior bedroom doors provides a directional cue to the resident. Without this type of identifying marking, the person may not be motivated to leave their room.

Josh's book, *The Dementia Concept*, contains much more in terms of his research into memory care. His cutting-edge training philosophy – understand, connect, engage -- pushes the dementia care industry forward.

With regard to the living quarters of memory care residents, the basic idea is to reduce danger without instituting limiting restrictions and to allow freedom for exploration in an environment of safety. For those in early stages of dementia, begin making small changes. Sweeping alterations in the living environment causes confusion. Start the process slowly.

With regard to design not only of memory care, but all spaces, Tuscan Gardens had the pleasure of working with Lisa Cini and her company Mosaic, as well as Suzanne Alford from LCS.

Mosaic's innovative approach engages every element of

design to create a complete environment – one that reflects the spirit, practical needs, and brand of each of their clients. Mosaic is renowned for its turnkey approach. Internationally known as a champion of innovative senior living and health care design, the firm also has won awards for its restaurant and corporate work.

The Mosaic team, led by CEO Lisa Cini, uses unique processes like The Clarity Compass and The Collaborative Blueprint to develop a deep understanding of their clients' businesses and how that knowledge should translate into a functioning space, as well as the messages that the environment needs to convey. The Cornerstone Assessment tool used by Mosaic can generate pro formas from scratch or develop a detailed, phased project plan. The Value Maximizer inventories clients existing resources, assesses further needs and creates a gap list, analyzing the best and worst supplier relationships and letting clients know where Mosaic can help negotiate better pricing and making recommendations for new partners that offer money savings. The Process Navigator tool allows Mosaic to relieve clients of the day-to-day stresses of construction, procurement, and installation until the project is completed.

SHADOW BOXES

One other thing worth mentioning with regard to memory care living quarters (or actually any living quarters for that matter) is the use of shadow boxes. Shadow boxes have been used right outside resident rooms in memory care communities: the idea being to fill the boxes with seasonal pieces, mementos, photos or other items to remind the resident of their youth and visual identification of "their" room.

Shadow boxes are a nice way to personalize an area, but can often be underutilized as they are seen as "labor intensive" on the part of families or caregivers. In some cases, residents have no family members to populate the boxes with keepsakes or pictures.

One senior living design firm, studioSIX5, based in Austin, Texas, has worked to "digitize" shadow boxes to allow everyone to be represented with this charming and personalized device.

The digital memory boxes created by studioSIX5 feature a touch screen panel as well as a frame around the panel that includes space for a room number. The look is sleek, professional and modern. The wireless nature of the box, which is connected to the cloud and managed by the caregiver, allows uploading of one or several photos to create a slideshow or collage. The studioSIX5 designers program the boxes based on motion sensors to activate (fading in/fading out) as the door is approached. The boxes also can be placed inside the residents' room (displaying the same images) as a nice décor piece. For memory care residents, this is especially important as it reinforces they are in the right room.

An additional benefit of digital boxes is that even old photos can be sharpened to provide more vibrant colors or saturation.

For residents whose families aren't involved, caregivers can take current photos or select stock imagery based on the resident's likes, heritage or background.

Shadow boxes in front of unoccupied rooms can be used to showcase artwork or photos from community activities. A shadow box in the lobby can broadcast community information like dinner specials, daily activities, the weather or local news.

The brains behind studioSIX5 believe that beautiful interiors celebrate life, increase marketability and improve occupancy rates for senior living communities. That's why those are the only interiors they create. In addition, studioSIX5 offers purchasing services that not only save clients money, but assure a faster and smoother installation process. They offer the following services:

- Interior design audit/assessment

- Interior design master planning

- Initial project branding and imaging concepts

- Interior programming

- Colors, materials, and finishes selections

- Furnishings selection and specification

- Decorative lighting selection

- Interior architectural detailing

- Project documentation

- Construction administration

- FF&E purchasing management and installation

AROMATICS MATTER

In closing this section, I'd like to touch briefly on the aromatics issue.

When you first walk into any type of environment, you are immediately hit with a number of sensory impressions: the visual look and feel, the lighting, the scent or fragrance, and so forth.

We did sales events across the country – in fact, in our heyday in 2008, we were doing some 230 sales events weekly. Two things mattered beside the quality of the presentations themselves, both of which we institutionalized: music which reflects sound, and aromatics which reflect scent. Walk into a hotel room that smells stale, dingy or old, and that is the response that you will get. Walk into a hotel room that smells fragrant, energetic and alive, and that is the response you will get.

Similarly, and even more importantly, aromatics need to be central to any senior living community at every level. Our sense of smell is directly tied to the emotion-processing area of the brain. In fact, 75% of emotions are generated by smell, according to a Millward Brown study. The response to scent is strong indeed, reportedly lifting moods and easing symptoms. It's no wonder that most people respond favorably to scents which include sugar cookies, chocolate chip cookies, apple pie, and pumpkin pie.

Here are some areas in which aromatics can impact the quality of life for seniors.

- Kitchen: Items that have aromatic quality and entertainment character can be handled in the kitchen and dining areas, and to the greatest extent in an open or exposed kitchen area. Those that need to be cooked that do not offer that support will be handled in the institutional kitchen. This is the first level of aromatic support.

- The second level of aromatic support is from a massive

commitment to horticulture both inside and outside a community. Horticultural separators can consist of dill, rosemary, basil and mint. In other words, plants need not simply be plants. Consider basing horticultural choices in favor of aromatic plants that provide freshness, scent and quality, in addition to culinary content.

• The third level consists of hard-wiring buildings themselves for aromatics. Any number of current systems on the market provide for the inclusion of aromatics into the HVAC system so they become systemic across the entire board.

ScentAir MENA has released two such systems: ScentWave and ScentStream. The ScentWave scent delivery system is ideal for creating ambient scent environments in any business setting. It uses a dry-air technology that releases fragrance without sprays, aerosols or heated oils. Adjustable duration and intensity settings make it easy to customize the scent output for any environment. The easy to maintain ScentWave offers multiple installation options and also:

• Provides coverage for typical business spaces up to 2,000 square feet

• Utilizes easy to install scent cartridges (of more than 1,600 quality scents) that last approximately 300 hours

• Offers a motion detection sensor

The ScentStream HVAC scent delivery system create ambient scent environments in larger settings. The advanced diffusion technology releases fragrance into existing heating and air conditioning ventilation systems without sprays, aerosols or heated oils. Adjustable duration and intensity settings make it easy to customize the scent output for any environment. ScentStream also:

• Provides coverage for areas with an air volume up to 300,000 cubic feet

- Includes 24-hour clock with variable cycle times

- Offers simple replacement of scent bottles - no messy pouring of oil

ScentAir is the market leader of in-store scent solutions for brands and retailers. Its patented systems help enhance environments, communicate brands and create memorable experiences. They give their clients the tools to sculpt their own unique environment, completing their customers' experience by engaging memory and emotions through the sense of smell. Scents and systems can be customized to reflect and complement any brand or environment.

ScentAir 's patented scent delivery systems were originally developed by a former Lockheed Martin rocket scientist who had become a Walt Disney "Imagineer." The first "Scent Blitz" was used to provide aromas for attractions and special events at Walt Disney World theme park in Orlando, Florida. Seeing potential in other applications, Fragrance Technologies was started in a garage in Windermere, FL in 1994, designing engineered scent system for motion rides, military simulators and special theater exhibits.

In 2000, the name ScentAir Technologies was adopted as the company's focus expanded to systems and services that were more easily deployed in retail settings. The aroma marketing revolution had begun. Four years later, the company relocated to its current home in Charlotte, NC fueled by additional investment from Connecticut-based venture capital firm Alerion Partners. ScentAir 's management, operations, sales, and product development teams have continued to grow and evolve. Strategic supply, sales, and distribution partnerships around the world ensure the company's continued status as scent marketing's pioneer and industry leader.

Creating distinctive and appealing fragrances is an art. ScentAir's fragrance oils are complex and specially formulated, using only the highest quality ingredients. ScentAir partners with the world's leading fragrance houses to create and deliver the most enticing, exotic aromas. These are the same fragrance houses that provide oils for many top perfumeries and aromatherapy providers. All of the scents have been tested to ensure superior quality.

As you can see with hardwiring buildings for aromatics in the way that ScentAir has, you are assured of not only building penetration, but also consistency with respect to the overall fragrance and scent of the entire building on a 24/7 basis. Tuscan Gardens is working to develop its own signature scent that is discernible and consistent from the front door and throughout.

HIGHLIGHTS

1. Larger private apartments and smaller common areas provide luxury on your own and intimacy within a group.

2. High ceilings and natural light contribute to a greater sense of size. Use ample windows for the greatest amount of natural light and high ceilings to provide a sense of verticality, both externally and internally.

3. Walls and halls do their part to create isolation. Natural dividers like potted palms or sculpture allow for private, although not disconnected, contact.

4. Open seating at all mealtimes enhances socialization, irrespective of the residents' natural tendency to focus in earnest on their conversation. Sitting with different people allows for new friendships.

5. Memory care presents its own set of design challenges and opportunities. Seek specific, professional guidance in designing these spaces.

6. Music and scent do their part to deliver an exceptional resident experience. Engage all the senses to achieve greater satisfaction.

CHAPTER 7

THE ART OF EATING

As they say in Italy, Italians were eating with a knife and fork when the French were still eating each other. The Medici family had to bring their Tuscan cooks up there so they could make something edible.
~ Mario Batali

As mentioned in the "Preface," we're Italian and, as Italians, eating is akin to breathing. A book on *The Art of Living* by any self-respecting Italian wouldn't be complete without a full chapter on food.

It is said that the average person will spend 15 years of their life eating and I'd be willing to bet that the average Italian could add at least a year or two to that figure.

Considering the substantial time invested in eating, the quality and variety of food, as well as the ambiance, should be equally meaningful. The high-energy "younger" senior has likely spent their working years experiencing fine dining. Therefore, any onsite dining should mirror the compelling offers and courteous treatment on the part of staff and management that you could find in any area fine dining establishment. Marrying interior design with vibrant menu selections will resonate and remind them of great dining experiences enjoyed during their life and on their travels.

With almost one million restaurants in the United States, senior living facilities may find that local dining establishments outside the community siphon residents from your restaurants. Those area restaurants are also competing for your staff's dining dollars as well. With the proliferation of options like free delivery and online ordering, you must be prepared with offers superior in taste, variety, and value in order to compete. The camaraderie inherent in and the convenience of the dining room can't be relied upon when it comes to persuading residents to enjoy in-house meals. The offer must be compelling enough to stand on its own. In addition, food and snacks brought in by residents or their friends and family eliminate the need to patronize your restaurants or community store.

It's necessary for senior living facilities to compete with not just delicious food, but pleasing aesthetics and exceptional service. By combining these elements, your community can create dining experiences that rival or surpass those of area restaurants and position your restaurants to be dining destinations for the families and friends of residents, as well. When you capture residents and their circle of friends, you gain a competitive edge that can't be copied.

Atmosphere is also key. Residents should be able to enjoy "jeans and T-shirt" casual dining in a place to hang with friends and grab a sandwich or drinks, but when the mood strikes a linen napkin and crystal experience should be available.

Interior design does its part to reinforce theming or a farm to table philosophy through use of a natural color palette and rustic materials. Regardless of the approach you choose, deliver any meals in an atmosphere of resident care and gracious hospitality.

Registered dietitians and executive chefs should collaborate over the initial establishment of a menu, using industry leading and lagging indicators to inform potential selections. Other intelligence gathering tactics include analyzing R&D reports from popular national brands that identify their top menu performers, benchmarking local restaurants (both independent and chains).

Understanding the marketplace, benchmarks and competitors, as well as residents' own intergenerational behaviors leads to identifying ideal menu items that complement your residents' wants and aligns them with trends and insights.

Menu categorization helps create a comprehensive dining selection with menu items separated into salads, soups, sandwiches, entrées, and desserts. Within each category, too, further segmentation into ethnic, wellness, and vegetarian selections aids residents in making meaningful choices.

The challenge is to serve with consistency a good, old fashioned home cooked meal, as well as grilled shark and sushi for the curious resident or friend visiting the community. Ideally, it's organic, healthy food brought fresh to the table – whether meat and potatoes or goat cheese on flatbread – that can be traced to a sustainable source and offered to everyone across the continuum, not just the more mobile residents.

A 2014 study by Ecolab described what residents want and expect in senior living communities, illustrating an increased expectation of hotel or resort-like amenities.

Expectations:

85% expect a coffee shop

82% expect a salad bar

78% expect a bakery or fresh baked items

76% expect bistro options

55% expect grab and go options

43% expect vegan or vegetarian options

39% expect an onsite bar or pub

37% expect gluten-free options

Wants:

85% want quality and variety of food

71% want meal delivery to their private living quarters

61% want onsite fine dining

Beyond meeting dietary requirements, ongoing menu development should incorporate resident preference and prevailing trends, including both familiar and exotic choices. A dining committee or dining survey allows residents to take ownership of any menu changes.

Dining committees should comprise a cross section of the community, incorporating the culinary team, residents, administration, and associates.

Initial committee meetings might suggest new flavors and tastes. The popularity of cooking shows and competitions on channels like The Food Network have impacted what people want, or want to try, when it comes to food. In addition to recognizable nutritional flavors, residents expect artistic presentation. On-trend foods and beverages they see on television create curiosity. If those choices also happen to have a traceable or ethical sourcing component, it's good food that residents also can feel good about.

Dining surveys further customize menus for your unique dining population, avoiding cookie-cutter solutions and putting in place a success formula that won't be easily replicated. Menu items drawn from surveys and discussion really resonate with residents.

Tuscan Gardens surveys its residents. They know our capabilities and our chef's specialties. In light of those, we issue a monthly survey to discover what new items the residents would like him to prepare. We incorporate those into a go-forward menu for the next 30 days. Menus are developed for a 90-day segment and published 30 days in advance. These quarterly menus are modified subject to resident feedback and may have inclusions, exclusions or modifications based on community preferences.

We also take customization one step further. The entry process to Tuscan Gardens includes an in-depth personal profile focused on each resident. This profile covers the big things: allergies, diet restrictions, as well as personal preferences such as brand of beer/wine or a desire for smaller portions. The profiles are intended for public display and posted in the kitchen. Keeping this information front and center creates learning opportunities about the residents.

"Create your own" dishes (i.e., salads, pizzas, flatbreads) seldom fail to delight. A good variety of choices helps solidify the feeling that this is their personal restaurant.

Keeping residents engaged is an important aspect of dining services. Offering tasty and eye-appealing food in attractive venues is not enough. You must continually market and promote your food and venues to increase resident participation in meals, ensuring daily nutrition and socialization.

In general today's resident exhibits a willingness to be more adventurous with ingredients, an openness to contemporary twists on traditional favorites and a curiosity to experience exotic flavors drawn from other cultures.

As you might expect, Tuscan Gardens makes liberal use of classic Italian recipes that stand the test of time as well as newly imagined traditional favorites that have been reworked into healthier options.

Also at Tuscan Gardens, we encourage residents to share favorite recipes from their personal collections. Recipes handed down through the family by word of mouth or on faded notecards become treasured keepsakes. By allowing residents to share, we promote socialization and recollection as they relive memorable times around the family dining table or in their own kitchens at home.

Menu suggestions developed during committee meetings can be turned over to the culinary team for analysis, including nutritional content and cost-effectiveness. This is not to say that current menu items aren't analyzed periodically as well. Ongoing analysis helps identify the most popular dishes and keeps your dining establishments ahead of the curve when it comes to food.

One way to introduce new menu items to the residents is through a tasting event, which is a wonderful way to create a festive and informative experience around food. Not only will you gain resident buy-in for the new dishes, you may be able to identify trends that will prepare you for upcoming dining desires.

Continually offering new menu items that reflect popular concepts and trends can boost participation and celebrate the diverse backgrounds of your residents. And don't forget that those new and trendy dishes, as well as the tried and true favorites should always be available. As mentioned in "Chapter 6: Interior Spaces" having all day/anytime dining or an "always available" menu (even if it's a scaled down version of your full menu) reinforces the fact that this community is the residents home and when you are at home you eat whenever you like.

At Tuscan Gardens, our philosophy is that while the kitchen does have a certain set of hours, we can accommodate our residents at any time. When the external Tuscan Kitchen is open, residents can walk in at any time, place an order and generally watch their meal made right before their eyes. If it's a late-night meal they are after, the kitchen manager utilizes the institutional kitchen to fulfill the request.

Menu development is another way that you can show consideration to your diverse resident base. Adding ethnic or regional dishes or alternate menu choices or simply printing large-print, pictorial, Braille or translated menus sends a clear message that everyone matters.

The last piece of the fine dining puzzle is exceptional service and management. The key to continuing satisfaction and a positive experience is responsiveness to the resident's needs. Courteous service is the type of treatment residents have come to expect at local restaurants and meals within their community should be no exception. If you have set the menu and the mood for unforgettable dining, complete the experience with a finely set table and gracious service.

There is a degree of aesthetic when it comes to china and flatware. Good food and elegant aesthetics cover a multitude of sins. While that doesn't mean you can get away with bad care, it does mean that a fine dining experience encourages residents to overlook the bumps in the road.

Further, many operational hiccups can be overcome by management being present and visible. Being in the right place at the right time can make all the difference, particularly if it's simply the manager walking around and chatting with residents during meal time. In this way, you establish an atmosphere of a high-end restaurateur ensuring his favorite "regulars" have everything they need.

COFFEE

The proliferation of Starbucks on every street corner should tell you that the coffee culture is firmly entrenched in today's society and seniors aren't excepted from this trend. Approximately 83% of adults drink coffee which translates into 400 million cups per day. Coffee lovers drink all day long, between and after meals, making "away from home" coffee the number one drink in the morning and the number two drink in the afternoon.

The fascination with frappuccinos, cappuccinos, and more shows no signs of slowing. It's estimated that specialty coffee and tea sales are increasing by approximately 20% every year, which should give any senior living community reason to consider installing a coffee cart, kiosk or café on premises.

The following describes the coffee experience progression in terms of hot beverages.

A **self-serve coffee station** allows residents to "pour and go." However, self-serve stations come with their own set of challenges. If choosing a self-serve option, the coffee must be fresh and consistently available. That means a staff member dedicated to monitoring. The prep station must be well stocked with napkins, stirrers and paper (not Styrofoam) cups. Premium condiments include milk (regular or skim), cream or half and half with either liquid or powder flavorings (vanilla, nutmeg, cinnamon or cocoa, to name a few)

Carts or kiosks are a nice bridge between self-serve and a full café. Carts must be staffed, but this allows some customization of beverages and interaction between servers and residents. Considering the survey cited above that 85% of residents expect a coffee shop, a cart may be an inexpensive compromise for some communities.

Cafés employ knowledgeable baristas who have the ability to create specialty drinks to a resident's detailed order, as well as share information on origin and traceability of ethically sourced beans, artisanal items or other unique features of the products on offer. Cafés tend to be coffee "destinations" rather than "grab and go." Residents frequent on-premises cafés due to the quality of products, level of service, and comfortable environment that encourages lingering a long time over a cup.

Cafés in particular offer a full coffee experience with a wide beverage range and vibrant atmosphere, which is why 68% of adults prefer to purchase coffee outside the home or workplace. Deliberate design allows cafés to appeal to all the senses. From the sound of frothing milk and light music to the smell of the richly brewed beans and to the sights of well merchandised "take home" items, the café experience fills competing needs for both camaraderie and calm.

The primary part of that experience is the personalizing of hot beverages, including individually brewed pour-over coffees, macchiatos or lattes made to order. Espresso machines are particularly popular. Surveys show that 64% of adults are satisfied with coffee options if an espresso machine is available vs. 41% who claim satisfaction in the absence of one.

Coffee drinkers are becoming more and more interested

in the sustainability issues related to coffee beans. Direct trade programs for sourcing single origin coffees remove the middlemen and allow individual growers to achieve economic stability.

This growing interest contributes to what's known as the third wave of coffee, a movement to recognize coffee as an artisanal item, like wine, rather than a commodity. Third wave concerns itself with high quality at all stages of production – growing, harvesting, and processing — through cooperative relationships with growers, traders, and roasters. Like wine, third wave coffee encourages appreciation of flavors, varietals, and growing region.

An on premises café also provides a wonderful opportunity to invite the community in and create a diverse experience. Some ways you can enhance community and generate revenue through your café are:

- **Educational Programs:** Morning tastings, brewing demonstrations and educational experiences around coffee-growing practices generate excitement.

- **Art Exhibits:** Exhibiting work from local artists brings culture into the café.

- **Live Entertainment:** A single troubadour enhances the relaxed atmosphere.

- **Merchandising:** Favorite coffee blends and specialty mugs extend the experience into residents' quarters and contribute to a marketplace feel.

HEALTHY DINING

Healthy dining has become a high priority for aging Americans. Information on nutrition is widely available and with the advent of technological "tracking" tools, it's never been easier to eat right. Current health and wellness trends include plant-based/meatless and natural dishes that use whole, less processed ingredients.

Healthy dining also has a lot to do with good communication and proper setting. Diners appreciate restaurants that provide nutritional information either onsite or online, as well as those that offer a "wellness" atmosphere of open/exposed kitchens, service lines showing ingredients, and natural décor of green or earthy tones.

Today's seniors expect a great variety of menu options and dining accommodations, as well as a lively "social atmosphere." Residents are more likely to attend meals if they feel that the community is observant of their health, social, and even religious dietary needs. With this in mind, dining facilities must accommodate a variety of preferences, with respect to the food itself as well as the ambiance of the dining spaces.

With the greater emphasis on wellness and in light of the survey showing residents want gluten-free, vegetarian, vegan, low sodium, and similar options, healthy ingredients should be emphasized in all menu items. That includes innovating traditional recipes with effective substitutions and right-sizing portions to make healthy eating easier. Chefs who honor the pure flavors and wholesomeness of the ingredients stay true to the recipes, but also serve the residents with the greatest nutrient value.

Basing the menu on in season fruits and vegetables, ideally harvested from an onsite garden, keeps residents engaged and the menu interesting. For anything that can't be sourced onsite, using local growers and traceable, ethical producers means "good for you" meals are also good for others, namely the environment and the community.

Some ways that culinary staff can control the level of calories, added fats (saturated and trans fats), sugars, cholesterol, and sodium, while maximizing the amount of fiber and essential nutrients include:

- Incorporating more vegetables, fruits, and whole grains in entrees to maximize nutrients and food volume, while controlling calories.

- Using low-fat dairy products, lean meats, poultry, fish, and legumes.

- Avoiding saturated fats.

- Substituting ingredients with similar ones that improve nutrition without sacrificing taste.

- ◆ *Replacing salt with fresh or dried herbs, citrus, vinegars, and spices enhances flavors in soups and stews.*

- ◆ *Reducing refined sugar and incorporating more fresh fruits and spices like cinnamon, nutmeg, and vanilla brings out sweetness in dessert items.*

- Using low-fat and healthy cooking methods to maximize flavor, quality and nutrition retention

  - ◆ *Roasting and broiling drip fat away from the food*

  - ◆ *Steaming retains the natural flavor of vegetables*

  - ◆ *Stir-frying and sautéing allow for rapid cooking with cooking spray, low sodium broth or a small amount of only vegetable based oils that are lowest in saturated fats such as canola or olive*

  - ◆ *Poaching (traditionally for fish or poultry) simmers in water or flavorful liquid (broth or vinegar), allowing food to retain shape and moisture without adding fat*

  - ◆ *Baking with covered cookware and added liquid to retain moisture*

SOFT DRINKS

Seniors are at a higher risk level for maintaining adequate hydration. With early intervention, residents at the greatest risk for dehydration can be identified and assisted. Fluid stations are a great way to ensure that hydration receives the attention it deserves and that all residents can easily take steps to remain well hydrated.

Placing fluid stations in common areas with large beverage dispensers reminds residents to drink up. Consider fruit infused ice water or even sweet, cool fruit juices. An impromptu smoothie bar mixes things up a bit and creates an opportunity for festivity and fun.

- Water: Filtered tap water, 100% fruit-infused, seltzer or flavored

- 100% Fruit juice

- 100% Vegetable juice (low sodium)

- Milk (unflavored and certified organic or rBGH-free)

- Non-dairy milk alternatives (unsweetened)

- Teas and coffee (unsweetened, with only naturally occurring caffeine)

Regardless of how you choose to promote hydration, remember to choose beverages that are locally sourced, sustainably produced, and organic when possible. Use tap or fountain dispensers and encourage residents to carry reusable cups or containers.

Sugar-sweetened beverages should be offered prudently. These include all sodas, fruit drinks (fruit juices or nectars with added sugar), sport drinks (especially those labeled for rehydration for athletes), low-calorie drinks, and other beverages that contain added caloric sweeteners, such as sweetened coffee/tea drinks, rice drinks, bean beverages, sugar cane beverages, horchata, and non-alcoholic wines/malt beverages.

Don't ignore beverage trends either. Seniors will want to feel that their food and beverage observes some of the more popular styles. According to Baum + Whiteman, the following represent 10 Beverage Trends.

1. House-made Sodas: Fruit, mint and citrus flavors

2. Fresh-pressed Juices: Green, beet, carrot, and more

3. Craft Coffee: Small batch, local roasters, organic, fair trade, and pour-overs

4. Botanicals: Herbal liqueurs, house-made bitters

5. Tea: Specialty ices, Thai, Southern, and in cocktails

6. Coconut Water: Fruit and liquor mixed

7. Mocktails: Non-alcoholic drinks with fruit and the aforementioned house-made sodas

8. Fermented Drinks: Kombucha, koji cocktails, bottle fermented

9. Beer-based Cocktails

10. Wine on Tap: Opened bottles tap preserved and chilled for longer use

"HARD" DRINKS

According to a University of Pittsburgh study, about 70% of assisted living residents drink alcohol and more than one-third indulge daily. Among independent living residents the figures are even higher. That's why a happy hour culture may work well in most senior living communities.

Some of the most popular alcoholic drinks among seniors include home brewed beers, craft cocktails (Bloody Marys, Margaritas, and Martinis often made with flavored spirits), themed or seasonal drinks for holidays and classics like Manhattans and Cosmopolitans.

GRAB AND GO

Adding a grab and go case benefits both residents and staff. Cold items like salads, sandwiches, wraps, or even ready-to-heat entrees made by the chef offer convenience, quality, and comfort when residents feel like staying in for an evening.

Hot ready-made foods like rotisserie chicken with all the sides takes the grab and go concept a step further. Imagine how pleased staff members will be after a long day at work to pick up dinner from the restaurant on their way out of the door.

Included in this category can be packaged ingredients or items served in the restaurant. Imagine selling your own line of coffees, teas or specialty condiments and sauces used in your recipes. See the merchandising section below to see how Tuscan

Gardens has leveraged this concept, including packaging popular recipes in a unique cookbook that allows residents' friends and family to enjoy the Tuscan Gardens experience in their own homes.

MEMORY CARE DINING

Fun and manageable meals will make dinnertime pleasant. Ensuring that meals for your memory care patients are easy to eat and capture attention leads to better nutrition. Consider leveraging more finger foods for residents who have difficulty holding utensils.

For those with swallowing issues, pureed food can be molded into recognizable shapes for a more appetizing look. Use dining scarves rather than bibs to protect clothes. They not only preserve your residents' dignity, but also signify the beginning and end of the meal.

When you increase engagement during mealtime for memory care residents you decrease frustration.

A NOTE ON STAFF DINING

Don't forget to promote your dining venues and meals among staff members as well. They are an important customer base, too. Proper nutrition on the part of team members contributes to cognitive performance and improves mental clarity, memory, energy, and focus. Plus, menu choices and attractive dining spaces help shape your company's image value, influence the overall workplace experience, and contribute to your unique corporate culture.

If you seek to position your workplace as forward-thinking and innovative, the environment (including dining areas) will either support or detract from that message. Considering the tight labor market, differentiating yourself to attract top talent by offering attractive food and dining spaces will convey your unique values and priorities.

According to a recent survey from provider association LeadingAge and dining services firm Unidine, dining staff turnover continues to be of great concern. Of 139 LeadingAge member respondents who do not outsource dining services, about 65% identified dining staff stability as a challenge. For those who do outsource, only 15% reported finding value in workforce stability through that partnership. Either way, attracting and retaining dining staff will continue to be an important function moving forward and a vibrant staff dining program can be a drawing card for your community.

Implementing technology, such as a mobile app, allows team members to spend their mealtime enjoying the food and not waiting in line. Your staff can order online, in advance, and have their meal ready when they are. Adding a "delivery" feature for your workers brings their food right to their desks. You can also leverage the app to notify diners (residents and staff) of daily specials, nutrition information, and more.

Use loyalty programs to increase participation and track popular products. Consider offering a small free product after a certain quantity has been purchased to create surprise and engagement. Easy payment options (like debit cards) allow staff to enjoy the same great food served to residents. Frequent diner punch cards encourage repeat business among your team.

MERCHANDISING

Merchandising and private labeling various items for sale solidifies the branding of any senior living community and differentiates it from its competitors. With a tagline like *The Art of Living*, it's imperative that Tuscan Gardens demonstrate that in very tangible ways and private labeling is one way we do that.

From a branding standpoint, private labeling affords you the opportunity to control the quality and the selection process. Plus, it gives you a wonderful sense of ownership in that this is "our brand" – our wine, our cheese, our olive oil. You are essentially branding components that allow others to identify products with you and your community.

With the advent of my former national business, we started private labeling and distributing wines to key community leaders and friends. The process went like this.

We taste tested wines from some of the best of the California growers until we came up with a Cabernet, a Merlot, and a Chardonnay to bottle for that particular year.

We then developed custom label artwork for each year which we then named the "Jordano" for the Cabernet, "Jared" for the Merlot, and "Isabella" for the Chardonnay (the names of our three children).

What we ended up with was exceptional wine that was less expensive than we could ever have bought in the wholesale marketplace and it was released with its own authentic original piece of art.

With that successful experience under my belt, I decided that Tuscan Gardens would do the same with respect to signature product lines that are associated with our essence and culture, such as:

- Cabernet

- Merlot

- Sangiovese

- Pinot Noir

- Red Meritage

- Chardonnay

- Pinot Grigio

- White Meritage

- Extra Virgin Olive Oil

- Balsamic Vinegar

- Parmigiano

- Romano

- Letterhead and Envelope Stationery for each guest

- Large Wooden Spoons

- *La Trattoria at Tuscan Gardens Cookbook*

Select private label items which are incorporated into the overall inventory available on property as well as for sale to families and friends. In addition, recipes will soon be published in the Tuscan Gardens Cookbook that reflect signature dishes which we provide in our community. As other private label opportunities present themselves over time, we will evaluate each and determine how the item fits within our culture and strategic goals.

To elaborate on the cookbook concept, when a community is being formed, a particular work product of that community is its own cookbook. In our case, it's a specific cookbook per community. La Trattoria of Tuscan Gardens at Venetia Bay versus La Trattoria at Tuscan Gardens of Palm Coast, for example. The cookbooks are made up of recipes submitted by residents and vetted by Tuscan Gardens chefs for use in our own menus. Beyond the basic recipe, however, is a story from the resident as to the reason behind the submission, whether it's a treasured family recipe or a dish discovered on world travels; each with its own special anecdote. The cookbooks are subject to continuous editions as our Tuscan Gardens family grows and changes.

Merchandising firmly dovetails into the current trend toward "craftsmanship." When the highest quality items are not only used onsite for menu items, but also packaged and offered for sale, you elevate your offerings to an artisanal quality and encourage their purchase by gourmands within the general public. From handmade sausages and salamis and artisan cheeses to fresh bakery items and made from scratch sauces, you create a dining and shopping destination within your own grounds that promotes your community to prospective residents and the world at large.

INNOVATIONS

Staying ahead of the curve when it comes to dining requires continual innovation. Some interesting initiatives we are considering or have adopted at Tuscan Gardens include:

- *Live from Tuscan Gardens:* A public access cooking show taped from the community that embraces the seasonality of food by preparing signature recipes cooked with herbs and produce harvested on site.

- **Chef's Table:** Having the chef dine with selected community members on an ongoing basis provides a cherished special event in the lives of residents. The "one-on-few" format encourages open communication as well as serves as a learning experience about menu development. This builds lasting relationships as well as loyalty to the community with this resident-pleasing activity.

The multi-course meal observes dining restrictions, if any, yet doesn't stint on the extras – fine china, crystal, and upscale flatware. Menus may be presented to residents in advance to allow the anticipation to build.

- **Cooking demonstrations:** Educational programs that focus on healthy cooking methods and preparation techniques tend to draw crowds. Chef presenters may include the in-house executive chef or guest chefs from local restaurants. Video screens placed above the cooking area project what's happening and allow everyone to follow along. This type of full sensory experience – smell, sound, sight, and tastes of the finished product – engages the residents. A take-home recipe card completes the experience.

A natural offshoot of cooking demonstrations is actually cooking classes, which let residents actively participate in the preparation. Hands-on learning coupled with dining on the "educational product" makes for a memorable afternoon.

"DINING DOLLARS"

Depending on the specific meal plans available, communities may offer one, two or three full meals per day. How those are "claimed" allows residents flexibility and choice.

For example, some communities allow the one meal option to be converted into a monthly allowance, in which the person may eat what, where, when and how much they desire. The resident may use the allowance in a "declining balance" type system to purchase a regular breakfast, lunch or dinner, or possibly direct it toward a special themed event (holiday meal, Sunday brunch, etc.).

The ultimate in freedom and flexibility is the opportunity to use dining dollars in unique ways and places such as in onsite

Farmers Markets or Village Stores, as well as with room service.

Declining balance programs are similar to the models of a traditional country club food and beverage fee structure. Declining balance meets the demand on the part of residents for variety, selection, quality, and value, as well as more complete access to and control over their funds.

For example, in some communities, residents are provided one meal per day and a continental breakfast. In some scenarios, residents must use their meal per day at the time of meal service or lose the value of the meal. This hamstrings residents into eating at the same time and place each day.

By using a declining balance program, a predetermined dollar amount per resident is set, based on current meal per day valuation. This is then credited to the resident's account at the beginning of the month and can be used in any and all dining venues on the meals they most desire. As purchases are made, accounts are debited and the balance declines. Menu pricing allows residents to select as many or as few items as they would like in the course of the day, paying only for what they order. The program is not unlike our son Jordan's "Eagle Bucks" program at Boston College.

Price points can be broken down by meal or course such as soup, entrée or dessert. Special events or premium dishes (filet mignon, lobster tail, etc.) may carry an "upcharge." The higher-end selections provide a chance for the culinary team to showcase their talents, as well as generate additional revenue.

Rolling over monthly meal values means residents can "bank" their dining dollars, perhaps for times when family or friends are visiting. However, meal value credits seldom transfer to cash, nor should they be deducted from the monthly fee. Upon depletion of the monthly meal value before month's end, the resident's account gets "charged" for additional meals, which then appear on the monthly statement.

Using declining balance in dining satisfies residents who want options while protecting the financial viability of a dining program. It establishes a level of certainty for planning purposes, allowing management to achieve efficiencies in purchasing and preparation. Food cost is more appropriately protected because residents pay for the items they select, which are priced based upon their actual cost.

THE ECONOMICS OF IT ALL

Hopefully, the foregoing has provided "food for thought" with regard to ways that dining can enhance *The Art of Living* and satisfy today's and tomorrow's senior. The challenge, however, is how can a service provider satisfy the more sophisticated palate in a cost effective and efficient way. Crafting forward-thinking menus with more exotic flavors is certainly not a cheaper option than the older "cafeteria-style" model.

The economic factors which drive price fluctuations in food include:

- Higher costs of farming, producing, and growing

- Natural disasters in growing areas such as droughts and floods, which may be linked to climate change or global warming

- Increased food waste

- Greater interest on the part of consumers with regard to organic food and sustainable farming

- A reduction in environmental footprint (greening)

- Sustainable practices such as recycling oils

- Transportation costs

Clearly these factors can be both positive and negative, driving prices up or down: many of which are out of anyone's direct control. That's why using tools to constantly monitor pricing allows you to respond to these economic factors and receive the best pricing available.

Some ways to do this include:

- Continuous review of the cost of goods to ensure food cost percentages remain within a certain range.

- Use of supply management expertise and resources to obtain best value for the proper portfolio of products.

- Watch current trends and commodity market indicators to determine any cost factors, as well as the monthly Consumer Price Index and Producer Price Index to monitor cost of goods.

- Review street selling price form comparative competitor research and surveys.

I can remember several years ago I had the idea that I wanted to package and market my mother's Sicilian Soup. Mom's Sicilian Soup is similar to the more widely known "Italian Wedding Soup", but twice as thick and delicious. I'd done my research into industrial kitchens and believed that this was a great concept. I even had planned out a television commercial in which my mother would speak in Italian, describing the soup – its origins, ingredients, and quality. I planned to retail the soup through the local grocery chain, Publix, and a few other select outlets.

However, after much number crunching, I just couldn't sell the soup affordably. To make it, to my mother's exacting standards and original recipe, it was just too expensive. The economics wouldn't support it.

I mention this in closing out the section because you will find that when it comes to your dining program you may need to be prepared to absorb an economic cost. If nothing else, it puts you in the position to recognize that your rental structure can absorb the additional cost. In the same way that some people buy a nice steak at the grocery for, say, $12 and cook it at home; there are others who pay $36 to eat that same steak at a fine restaurant. Know to whom you are marketing and the ones prepared to pay the sort of rental that delivers the fine restaurant experience.

As one of the great pleasures in life, food and the dining experience hold a special place in a resident's schedule. Depending on your demographic, whether it's the cultured, well-traveled and sophisticated Baby Boomer or the meat-and-potatoes loving member of the Silent Generation, you can deliver the resort style experience everyone loves with five-star meals and first-class service.

HIGHLIGHTS

1. Dining surveys customize menus for your unique dining population. By avoiding cookie-cutter solutions, you're putting in place a success formula that won't be easily replicated.

2. Introduce new menu items to residents through a tasting event, which is a wonderful way to create a festive and informative experience around food.

3. Adequate hydration is of special concern for seniors. Strategically placed drink stations help ameliorate that concern.

4. Healthy cooking techniques maintain flavor without adding salt, sugar or fat.

5. Implementing staff dining programs leads to greater participation in your food program and increased satisfaction on the part of associates.

6. Merchandising items that are identifiable with your community solidifies branding and delights residents and prospective residents.

CHAPTER 8

BRINGING THE OUTSIDE IN

Every time I imagine a garden in an architectural setting, it turns into a magical place. I think of gardens I have seen, that I believe I have seen, that I long to see, surrounded by simple walls, columns, arcades or the facades of buildings – sheltered places of great intimacy where I want to stay for a long time.
~ Peter Zumthor

In the same way the full premises of a senior living community serve as the entirety of a resident's living quarters, so too should the exterior and the grounds be an extension of the living area.

ENTRIES AND PARKING

In general, the exterior of the buildings themselves reinforces the authenticity spoken about in "Chapter 5." For example, the entry to Tuscan Gardens does have a type of porte-cochere for the receiving of residents and guests simply because it is functionally necessary, but it's minimized as much as possible, because the look we want to achieve is that of a normal residence to the greatest extent possible, albeit a rather grand entrance. After all, when is the last time you went to someone's private home that had that type of external cover? Whether British mansion, castle or Tuscan villa, you generally won't find a drive-through.

Unlike a private residence, senior living communities require an ample parking area. Cars are a necessary evil in that they provide for transportation, both for visitors and staff. Unfortunately, they also are dissociative and incongruent.

121

Parking lots are even worse, because they not only exponentialize the incongruity, but they also render it static, so that it freezes that exponentialized incongruity for someone to actually experience. You can understand then, why, when conceptualizing Tuscan Gardens, I didn't want our residents experiencing it.

The answer, at least for us, was a substantially secluded parking area that was separated as much as possible from the main functional living areas by landscaping and site planning. Naturally, pickup and drop-off areas had to be accommodated as well as handicapped parking, which required some parking. However, absent that minimal contact, Tuscan Gardens worked to ensure that cars and parking lots were completely segregated and hidden.

What that means in practicality is that minimal parking is available in the front of the building, with very little parking visible from the main entry.

Lush vegetation, beyond making the grounds look spectacular, does double duty in screening parking areas. Parking lots are sequestered behind vegetation that surrounds the primary building, walkways and gardens, and are separated by its own level of landscaping.

Still, the parking lot is accessible either directly for those individuals who do not need to be dropped off or accessively after they have dropped off. For pick-up purposes, they would be accessible for pick up after they had left the parking lot area.

SITE CONSIDERATIONS

Other exterior accents at Tuscan Gardens, in addition to being pleasing to the eye, serve to cement the iconic look of our community. The magnolia trees lining the perimeter of the property not only create separation, but also identify to the visitor or resident that they have entered a unique living environment.

Further the properties are fenced in by an architectural palisade, fulfilling the need for architectural identification, as well as security. The palisade is high enough to provide no possibility for ingress or egress by anyone who is not otherwise authorized, yet still maintains a sense of design that aligns with Tuscan Gardens' theming and philosophy.

HORTICULTURAL FEATURES

From the standpoint of the exterior of a community that is to be used and enjoyed by residents, extensive gardens do double duty in being both visually pleasing and providing ample opportunity for activity. This is not to imply the interior holds no horticultural or botanical features, but rather that they are leveraged to an even greater extent out of doors.

Horticultural features need not be reserved to shrubbery, shade trees or hedges, but to the entire gamut of presentation – from raised boxes and potted plants to garden beds and even mini-orchards – of all manner of vegetation. That means flower and herb gardens, vegetable plots, and groves of fruit trees.

Because "gardens" is part of our name, Tuscan Gardens' overall horticultural approach is one of our primary differentiators. One of Tuscan Gardens' strategic imperatives is to support itself, on a self-sustaining basis, with nothing but its own organic growth in terms of fruits, vegetables, and herbs. That requires a great depth of productivity coming from the gardens. Considering space availability, this requires some creative landscape design that maximizes the amount of organic growth. While we may never be totally self-reliant, it's important to share our commitment to this goal. Cultivating our grounds fills an aesthetic need, but, as importantly, a practical and functional need as well. Sustainability through agriculture is part of the fabric of who we espouse ourselves to be and not a cute subscript for a marketing brochure.

Beyond that, the gardens play an important part of daily life where residents have the opportunity to grow their own fruit, vegetables, and herbs and participate in meal planning, preparation, and designing, at their option. The grounds have fountains on the property and are encircled by Magnolia trees, secured walkways, and an attractive palisade.

HYDROPONICS/AEROPONICS

One way that Tuscan Gardens can fulfill its stated objective to be self-supporting with produce is through hydroponics or aeroponics. In these types of growing situations, fruits and vegetables are grown without soil, utilizing air, water soluble nutrients, and light.

Hydroponics is the process of growing plants with their roots submerged in water. Aeroponics is a plant-cultivation technique in which the roots hang suspended in air while nutrient solution is delivered to them in the form of a fine mist.

With space always at a premium, hydroponics and aeroponics are a particularly attractive option for senior living communities in that growing systems tend to be designed in vertical columns. By no means above, one such company, AERO Development Corp, offers mobile gardens, wall gardens, and kitchen gardens for commercial and residential use. Each system consists of a vertical housing unit that dispenses nutrient-rich water through a distribution cap at the top of the unit to the grow cups staggered on the sides of the columns or panels. The grow cups house the plants in a bed of rockwool that allows the roots to grow unencumbered down the center of the column. Rockwool is a spun molten rock medium that promotes growth and nutrient absorption.

The nutrients in the water are those that are also found naturally in healthy soil. The AERO grow systems recycle the nutrient from a reservoir tank, conserving water, while giving the plants the needed nutrients on intermittent cycles.

This type of soil free growing offers the benefit of freshly grown food with no weeding, tilling, kneeling or getting dirty and uses less nutrients and water than traditional growing.

Many varieties of vegetables, herbs, and fruits can be grown hydroponically, including bibb lettuce, Swiss chard, tomatoes, basil, peppers, kale, arugula, oregano, chives, and parsley.

AERO has several different sized units for residential and commercial systems utilizing aeroponic technology for growing vegetables and fruits of all kinds.

For example, the AERO Mobile Garden has 72 grow cups and small casters for easy movement. This unit is ideal for rooftop or patio growing. The AERO Mobile Garden grows plants in less time than it takes in soil. Price per cup is about $18. Considering that organic lettuce can retail at $2.99 per head, you can grow approximately $125 worth of lettuce at once. Indoor growing can be accomplished with a light kit. The AERO Wall Garden has 41 grow cups. The AERO Kitchen Garden has 12 grow cups and can grow food right on your kitchen table.

For individuals or companies wishing to produce food on

a larger scale, AERO has year-round portable mini greenhouses (size 8x12 or larger) outfitted with an AERO grow system. For commercial greenhouse growing systems, AERO has turnkey installations that range from 2,400 square feet and up. These are "gutter connect" greenhouses that can be expanded to meet greater needs.

All come complete with heating and ventilation systems and the necessary controls. A number of external finishes and options are available to tailor the exterior to fit the user's unique environment.

Grower's Mini Greenhouse features aluminum framing and 15-year polycarbonate and is perfect for a small backyard system. Standard sizes of 6x8 to 10x20 are available.

The Hobby Mini Aeroponics Greenhouse is built from a treated lumber frame and includes a 15 year polycarbonate and a 32-inch screen door. Gardener's Mini Greenhouse is beautifully designed for growing aeroponically during most of the year.

FARMERS MARKET

As an aside, whatever is not produced on our property is intended to be locally sourced and certified as "farm to table." Should we ever get to a point that we overproduce, an onsite Farmer's Market would work as a community outreach, an opportunity to market our community and as a resident enrichment activity.

According to Projects for Public Spaces, the number of Farmers Markets in the United States has increased by 150% to approximately 7,000. By providing an onsite Farmers Market that offers produce grown on premises or items from area farmers, you extend healthy eating into residents' own living quarters and into the homes of your staff members, as well.

Staff, in particular, appreciate the convenience of being able to pick up fresh food items to share with their families. In addition to healthy produce, Farmers Markets that offer eggs, bread, and other specialty items such as pastas, vinegars, honey, and cheeses create an event-like environment. Offering samples to taste encourages purchases. Consider the following to add to the festive fun:

- Fresh-baked breads, such as pita, flatbreads, baguettes, and rolls.

- Cheeses and oils.

- Classic and exotic spices and herbs, as well as gourmet salts.

- Live or recorded music to enhance the shopping experience.

Depth of commitment to fresh foods requires staffing of an appropriate knowledge level: a master horticulturist at a minimum, leading a team of gardeners. Bringing in a local Home Depot or Target to "start things off" isn't going to cut it. A master horticulturist understands how to create and support enough basil, dill, rosemary, peppers, tomatoes, squash, eggplant, lettuce, corn, artichokes, blueberries, strawberries, lemons, oranges, figs, and olives to be not necessarily sustainable, but adequately reproductive to make a serious difference. Further, after further this type of person understands growing seasons to truly maximize both time and space.

TUSCAN GARDENS' HORTICULTURAL PHILOSOPHY

1. **We are fundamentally self-sustaining.**

2. **We are organic to the maximum practicable level and locally sourced beyond that.**

3. **The use of organic food and healthy recipes is part of our DNA.**

ORNAMENTAL GARDENS

Fruits and vegetables notwithstanding, some gardens serve the purpose of being places of relaxation, repose and contemplation, such as rose, orchid, butterfly or hummingbird gardens. These can either be identified as part of the overall garden landscaping or incorporated into private sanctuaries, as they are at Tuscan Gardens.

Tuscan Gardens "embeds" private sanctuaries into the landscaping, which provide for different styles of outdoor seating, encouraging meditation or quiet reflection.

All garden areas can be bordered or crisscrossed by walking paths. Walking paths should be secluded by landscaping as much as possible to achieve an environmentally rich experience. Anyone walking on a walking path shouldn't be able to see anybody outside of the property. To a resident, the only thing that should matter is on the property. Whether indoors or outdoors, everything that is important is happening inside the property, not outside the property. Landscaping needs to support that.

SPECIAL EVENTS

A robust outdoor program provides many benefits to any senior living community. Beyond growing delicious and healthy fruits and vegetables or fragrant flowers to brighten the vista, the great outdoors is a wonderful setting for special events.

Tuscan Gardens is planning two very distinct special events centered around nature's bounty. The first, the Festival of First Planting, celebrates the beginning of the growing season. Residents are encouraged to invite family, friends, and referrals to join in the festivities, which begins with sowing vegetable seeds that will one day be reaped and used in Tuscan Gardens' kitchen. While residents and guests can enjoy planting peppers and tomatoes, their efforts are supplemented and supported by master horticulturalists who are doing the heavy lifting. The day culminates with a casual barbecue and live music.

As you might expect, the second event is Fall Harvest when the frenetic activity of the spring comes to fruition in delicious and healthy fruits, herbs, and vegetables. Much more than a genial get-together, Fall Harvest signifies the changing climate as summer gives way to autumn. Again, residents, family, and friends are invited to harvest the produce that has reached the peak of maturity. Live music and *al fresco* cooking by the chefs, with many items that moments before were on the vine, punctuate the festivities.

Both of these and other special events at Tuscan Gardens are intended to be opportunities not only for residents, but for the community at large. The intended opportunity in this type of outreach is to make it clear what this lifestyle looks like.

Tuscan Gardens has the opportunity to be viewed as a community asset: by that, I mean the broadest possible meaning of community — not only the residents and their families, but our associates and their families, as well as members of the general public in the areas in which we operate.

I'm reminded of when Orlando was wrestling with the idea of rebuilding the Amway Center, our local events center and home to the NBA team, the Orlando Magic. The Amway Arena, its predecessor, was completed in 1989 at a cost of $110 million, entirely publicly financed. In 1991, it was voted "Arena of the Year" by Performance Magazine and nominated for "Best Indoor Concert Venue" in the Pollstar Concert Industry Awards. The intimate atmosphere allowed for upper bowl spectators to still be relatively close to the floor, due to near 50-50 split of upper bowl and lower bowl seats. The luxury boxes were near the ceiling.

Within a few short years, the Orlando Magic's ownership, led by Amway billionaire Richard DeVos, began pressuring the city for a new arena. Finally, toward the end of September 2006, city government and the Orlando Magic announced an agreement on the new arena, which would cost around $380 million with an additional $100 million for land and infrastructure.

At the time, the media and general public slammed the deal, pronouncing that the "rich get richer." I felt this was an unfair portrayal of what was happening and wrote an editorial asking citizens to look at the situation from both sides. Certainly it would be a place the local NBA team would call home. However, once built, it's also an asset for the community to take advantage of in terms of concerts and events.

Modestly, I'd like to think of some of the Tuscan Gardens common areas as an outreach asset for the community, certainly on a much smaller scale than a professional basketball court. There's absolutely no reason we can't hold continuing education seminars in the media room for professional caregivers in the area or host certification programs for therapists — which we do. The performance kitchen is an ideal location for cooking classes and educational programming centered on eating well.

By permitting "appropriate" programming on our premises for the resident community as well as the broader community, which consists of friends, family, referrals, and local citizenry, we promote Tuscan Gardens' reputation as a family which cares about the health and wellbeing of our residents and the people living in our surrounding area.

Before closing this chapter on the "great outdoors," one non-horticultural component of the grounds bears mentioning.

Functioning fountains provide a pleasant auditory venue for the movement of water, as well as a scenic design feature. Fountains outside the norm also provide iconic imagery for any senior living community. Tuscan Gardens is intended to employ two fountains on the grounds of each of its sites to fill just those functions.

We have actually imported the cleansing waters of Montecatini for use in and around the water features in the garden areas of Tuscan Gardens. Not only does that offer a light, cleansing, refreshing component of Italy itself, it suggests rejuvenation in *The Art of Living*.

HIGHLIGHTS

1. Secluding and segregating large parking areas give the feeling of a private, albeit large, residence, rather than a "facility."

2. Well landscaped grounds set the mood and shield residents from the stresses and strains of the outside world.

3. Hydroponics or aeroponics allow even the most landlocked community an opportunity to serve fresh produce in their dining rooms.

4. Farmers markets are great ways to share the bountiful harvest from the gardens on your grounds, but also serve as a marketing outreach.

5. Large gathering rooms within senior living communities can serve as extensions of the larger metropolitan community through holding continuing education seminars, certification programs, cooking classes or educational programming.

6. Functioning fountains provide several benefits, including a pleasant auditory diversion from the movement of water and a scenic design feature.

CHAPTER 9

THE RESIDENT EXPERIENCE
CREATING PURPOSE, PASSION & JOY

No one can avoid aging, but aging productively is something else.
~ Katharine Graham

The snapshot of today's senior is less a single photograph and more of a montage. Where in the past, seniors, as a group, seemingly lacked individual identifying characteristics to the point of being a single, faceless minority—a silent, snowy-haired army shuffling down the halls of ubiquitous "retirement homes." With the waves of Baby Boomers entering retirement (some 10,000 per day beginning January 1, 2011 and continuing for 19 years into the future), what it means to be a senior is being redefined.

The stereotypical "senior" no longer exists. Today's senior represents myriad backgrounds and beliefs. How and where they will age depends largely on what is available in the marketplace, in terms of environment and social offerings, and how this resonates with them and their desired aging experience. Nowhere will this be more keenly felt than in the amenities that make up the resident experience.

Boomers are accustomed to and are adept at forcing radical social changes. They did it as teens, young adults, and into middle age. The tsunami wave of retiring boomers or those contemplating retirement (79 million people or one quarter of the total U.S. population) are driving the senior living industry rather than the other way around.

As a group, Boomers are staying healthier and living longer

131

than past generations of seniors. Certainly improvements in health, nutrition, and medicine have contributed to this trend. Life expectancy is on the rise and continuing to trend upward. Global life expectancy in 1990 was approximately 64 years of age. That figure moved to 70 in the past 20 years with some estimates as high as age 80 by the year 2050. We have no reason to believe any regression will take place as medical science and biomedical technologies become ever more sophisticated.

The Senior Living industry finds itself in an enviable position of having an ever-widening target market, but also a challenging position of having to accommodate hugely varying needs across a vast age spectrum, from 65 to centenarians and everything in between.

Whether you call them "young seniors" and "old seniors" or refer to them generationally—Baby Boomers, the Greatest Generation, and the Silent Generation—these groups have radically different needs and preferences when it comes to aging, not the least of which is embodied in how they view themselves.

Boomers, in general, eschew all the traditional earmarks of aging — aluminum walkers, hospital beds and melamine cafeteria trays. Boomers are rewriting the definition of what it means to be a senior. The new definition will encompass technology and health and wellness, among other things.

The truth of the matter is Boomers don't see themselves as old. According to a Pew Research Survey, 61% of Boomers report feeling approximately nine years younger than their chronological age. The typical Boomer doesn't believe old age begins until about age 72... at least, that is, until the typical Boomer reaches that age!

And, actually, a typical Boomer is a misnomer. There is nothing typical about the population coming of retirement age today. The diverse and multi-cultural population crossing the age 65 threshold (my age as I write this book) belongs to varying races, cultures, and beliefs that will place a higher demand on senior living communities than ever before. Approximately 20% of current seniors are not Caucasian and 10% are foreign born. Three million people over the age of 55 identify as LGBTQ and that number is expected to double over the next two decades.

Every senior, regardless of background, has the obvious right to live well. It's up to the senior living communities to support these diverse preferences either within communities as a whole or by catering to subgroups within the larger community.

Certainly senior living communities exist that target groups based on background, culture, religion, social groups, and lifestyle, but perhaps more common are those that seek to address diversity through multilingual staff and regional or cultural menu items and events.

These vast differences in background, heritage, culture and more challenge senior living providers to create tailored experiences for high volume, wildly dissimilar audiences.

Emphasis in the two-word term resident experience rests more on the latter word, than the former. Today's seniors seek an experience rather than a simple commodity. Indeed, we have become an experiential economy in terms of many facets of life. Were it not so, there would be no need for business class or first-class airline travel. Using the preceding example, transforming a commodity—in the case of flights, getting from Point A to Point B—to an experience—getting from Point A to Point B with linen napkins and china plates—is the future of travel *and* senior living.

Not only will experiences become more personalized, but preferences will be monitored and recorded by the experience providers for future reference. Along the lines of "cookies" in your computer, providers will track everything you enjoy from types of food and drink to entertainment and amenities in order to serve them up time and again.

Experience design of this nature elevates simple products and services to memorable moments with the accompanying higher price tag. It's why Walt Disney World's Magic Kingdom commands a $100 per day entrance fee vs. the county fair at one-fifth of that figure. At its most basic, both share the same mechanics—spinning, rolling, floating—however, the former spins you through a world where Johnny Depp in full Jack Sparrow regalia commandeers your ship and a life-sized Abraham Lincoln rises to his feet and speaks with you.

The resident experience truly is the heartbeat of the whole Art of Living movement. The Tuscan Gardens mandate is to create a life of purpose, passion and joy. To that extent, we need to understand all the possible levels in this senior living life experience.

With all due respect to Abraham Maslow and his hierarchy

of needs, you can certainly see how senior living communities in all their various permutations move through these basic levels with their offerings.

1. Biological and Physiological

2. Safety

3. Love and Belonging

4. Esteem

5. Self-Actualization

The main objective of many senior living communities is to give elders a place to live and eat, which is fundamentally "warehousing" these individuals. Of course, government regulations also ensure that the second level, safety, is included.

The more enlightened communities, and those that I have had the pleasure of visiting and studying, see something beyond keeping seniors healthy and well, but add elements that lead to fulfillment, satisfaction, purpose, and joy. It's about identifying the higher goal or purpose for creating the community. Safety, shelter, and nourishment are obvious. People expect clean, well-lit environments. That's obvious. Today's seniors are asking: What else?

Lynne Katzmann, President and CEO of Juniper Communities, in speaking with Senior Housing News, talked about rebranding to share excitement, but also to combat ageism and widen market size. Katzmann notes that switching "from a description of features and benefits to define our product to thinking in terms of outcomes, what your life can look like."

How does your community answer that question? When a prospective resident or a decision maker crosses your threshold, what do you say? You'll get a wonderful place to live where you can eat gourmet food. You'll live in safety while others attend to your health and well-being. We'll achieve this through a combination of environment and care that positively impacts you on physical, psychological, mental, and spiritual levels. The result is a life of purpose, passion, and joy that delivers the very depth of personal satisfaction in the life you live.

That's certainly what we are trying to accomplish at Tuscan Gardens. Tuscan Gardens is fully focused on creating a resident experience that doesn't simply address those factors which relate to physical and psychological well-being, but to address those factors which offer the opportunity for purposeful and joyful expansion.

When I first started in the senior living industry, people were talking about the hospitality model. That was seen as the pinnacle of the resident experience. That's when we began asking about pushing that even farther to a concierge model, which is essentially hospitality on steroids.

When we understood that was the model for which we were striving, we made the conscious decision to align around that concept in every area – architecturally, interior design, programmatically, food, activities, and enrichment.

With this emphasis on experience in mind, all components of day-to-day senior life had to be evaluated through an experiential lens. *The Art of Living*, for example, demands an examination of food as nourishment, but also food as an aspect of fellowship and fun. The move is beyond basic needs to improved and innovated offerings, beyond service delivery to experience delivery, which allows for customization at several levels and monetizing those experiences that exceed the basic. Industry leaders must understand their current customers, their future customers and how what they offer dovetails into the expected or desired lifestyle.

Smart senior living providers will focus on building exciting offers based on retail excellence. These upscale experiences hold the potential to generate additional revenue. Rather than "nickel and diming" residents, the value-rich experiences will thrill residents and create the desire for them to immerse.

Of course, this all implies that the customers understand themselves and their expected or desired lifestyle, and with Baby Boomers that may still be in flux. Those who have spent the majority of their lives being trendsetters may still be unsure about "how" to be a senior. What do you do during the day? Senior living is less about a place to fade away and more about a place to live. Those of us in the senior living industry have a golden opportunity to assist them in defining and setting these expectations, which ideally dovetail into our own offerings.

CONSULTING ORGANIZATIONS

For those senior living communities that want to provide an exceptional resident experience, but may not necessarily know how to go about that, several consultancy organizations exist to offer either expertise or amenities or both. Masterpiece Living and PS Lifestyle are two examples.

Masterpiece Living is a multi-specialty group that is committed to older adults aging in a better way. To accomplish this, they forge partnerships with like-minded organizations. Masterpiece Living partners with organizations to maximize the potential of older adults. By aligning itself with visionary organizations who want to remain leaders in their respective markets, Masterpiece Living is creating destinations of successful aging.

The group grew up as the direct application of a research study that changed aging forever – The MacArthur Foundation Study on Aging. That landmark ten-year study by the MacArthur Foundation shattered the stereotypes of aging. It showed that 70% of physical aging, and about 50% of mental aging, is determined by lifestyle...the choices made every day. Rather than being a process of steady decline, aging can be a time of growth if seniors maintain physical and mental skills, reduce risk for disease and injury, and stay productive and engaged with life.

Masterpiece Living (MPL) offers today's senior living communities a strategic approach to successful aging. MPL partners with senior living and active adult communities, senior centers, cities, and healthcare organizations.

More than a wellness program, MPL is a cultural approach to successful aging based on the belief that more is possible when it comes to aging. With researched-based initiatives that build a more satisfied community, the end result is more satisfied residents and associates with lower risks for decline. MPL is the MacArthur Foundation Study on Aging brought to life, offering trademarked tools and techniques that measure and inspire aging community culture.

Research-based and rigorously tested, MPL focuses organizations on the priorities of healthy aging, creating new benchmarks that measure the improvement of individuals and the successful aging environment as a whole. The MPL team has over 300 years collective experience in the multiple aspects of aging science.

The research on aging shows how people age is mostly dependent on lifestyle, the choices the individual makes, and this knowledge has created a new older adult. Both motivated and empowered by this widespread knowledge, the new older adult tenaciously seeks resources, services, and living environments which enhance growth and promote independence. Recent AARP and International Council on Active Aging surveys confirm the emergence of the new older adult. MPL, as the direct descendant of the research on aging, is focused like a laser on these new aspirations of growth and potential. Partnering with MPL can help senior living organizations attract the informed older adult and continually engage their current population.

MPL works with leading experts in the field of aging. MPL also brings its partners reliable health information and health improvement tools from Mayo Clinic, and integrates their expertise into the MPL initiative.

Masterpiece Living has a proven track record of success. Everything it offers is based on solid research and has been pilot tested for soundness and usability. It places the journey as the top priority. A specific older adult in the partnership, or the actual community, or organization who partners, decides where they want to go on the journey to successful aging. MPL provides the guidance, the structure, resources and aging expertise, remaining with them for the whole trip, not just the beginning.

Much more than a program, MPL is a continually evolving culture. New research, the feedback from older adults and partner communities, and aging services industry developments, guide them in refining their approach and resources. Their stated objective is to remain at the forefront of the aging transformation in this country and others.

MPL has built an ever-growing network of over 70 visionary communities and organizations who are all part of the movement to change how aging takes place in this county for current older adults and for their grandchildren. The well documented approaches and the outcomes collectively achieved are part of a powerful developing case for changing public policy on aging.

Completely customized to an organization's need, MPL continually engages leadership, staff, sales and marketing, and older adults in the strategic effort, inspiring growth for all individuals.

Masterpiece Living provides its partner organizations with resources such as:

- **Measurement Tools** – Measure successful aging for residents and associates with research-based, piloted, and validated tools. Each participant receives customized reports that track their progress over time, and compare results to guidelines in current research and national norms. A mix of self-reported and objective measures, the Masterpiece Living Reviews assess physical health, social engagement, meaning and purpose, intellectual challenge, health risks, and mobility. Personalized reports and the follow up process are designed to empower individuals in making positive lifestyle choices.

- **Outcome Tracking** – Track organizational outcomes and create successful aging benchmarks that measure the engagement of the population and the successful aging culture. Utilize the aggregate measurement to track overall health and target specific needs. Establish Core Measures of Masterpiece Living that assess and provide standards of evolving a successful aging culture.

- **Integration Road Map** – Customize a process and a strategic approach designed to continually engage leadership, associates, and residents. The Integration Process provides the platform to unite and coordinate already-existing initiatives while helping to expand services offered.

- **Programs** – Nine research-based and piloted programs that support a culture of successful aging, representing over 650 hours of development. The programs can be implemented as a short-term campaign or seamlessly integrated into existing programs.

- **Resources** – The MPL secure website contains reports, programs, best practices, materials, training modules, newsletter articles, and other resources that maximize an organization's efficiency in delivering high quality initiatives.

- **Positioning and Branding** – Partners gain access to messaging, materials, marketing events, education, and presentations that articulate and demonstrate the advantage of being a MPL partner community. The MPL measurement, programs and resources can help attract and retain future clientele.

- **Education and Training** – Through MPL's Masterpiece Academy, partners receive comprehensive education for community leaders, all associates and older adults. Training modules, resources, E-Academy Videos, and supportive programs are designed to engage all associates and older adults in the movement of successful aging.

- **Networking** – MPL provides partners with access to best practices in programming, wellness, sales and marketing, and strategic planning through calls, webinars, an extensive website of resources, and an annual Lyceum.

PS Lifestyle is a national leader in providing exceptional amenity service and lifestyle solution experiences for mature adults.

Launched in August 2008, PS Lifestyle began with one simple goal – transforming senior community "beauty shops" into professional salons and spas. In embarking on this path, the minds behind PS Lifestyle learned that every service provided had three customers: a senior, a family member, and the senior community itself.

Today, PS Lifestyle's expanded, innovative portfolio of Salon & Spa, Shop, Magazine and Enrichment initiatives simultaneously caters to all three audiences boosting the marketability of its partner communities and enhancing resident and family satisfaction.

PS Lifestyle has a passion for enhancing the culture and dignity of many by defining and delivering lifestyle enrichment for the individual. PS Lifestyle initiatives reach beyond the walls of their partner communities to engage and delight mature adults, families and friends, professional caregivers, and industry partners.

PS Lifestyle's operations energize the physical, intellectual, and emotional wellness experiences of their clients, in turn providing peace-of-mind to families and giving its partner communities an unparalleled competitive edge. PS Lifestyle prioritizes and invests in relationships with residents, families, caregivers, and staff at each partner community. Tailored solutions include organized census building marketing initiatives, community web-based tools and significant investments in salon and spa.

PS Lifestyle's portfolio of offerings includes:

- PS Salon provides a true salon and spa experience to residents of more than 500 communities in 31 states. It offers the resources and experience of a national operating platform coupled with the personalized and caring attention of beauty professionals. Given the personal nature of the services provided, PS Lifestyle's 700+ employees develop deep and sensitive connections with their senior clients and, by extension, their families and professional caregivers. Since its founding, PS Lifestyle has paid attention to and learned from its unique experiences within the senior community environment, and has developed new innovations to complement its trusted position as the largest amenity service and lifestyle operator in the national marketplace.

- PS Shop is the only online destination where families and friends can personally connect with community residents by purchasing salon, spa & wellness services, pro-aging lifestyle products, and personalized gift certificates. Shop customers appreciate the platform's ease of access and many communication features, especially the email confirmations sent after every purchased service is delivered. Having facilitated tens of thousands of connections to date, PS Shop complements and amplifies its partner communities marketing and communication efforts.

- PS Magazine is a pro-aging lifestyle magazine designed for and about seniors. All 68 pages of each issue are printed in large, easy-to-read font on non-glossy, grip-able paper. Published bi-monthly and distributed for free to community residents, PS Magazine features:

  - *Exclusive interviews from cultural icons*

  - *Content from experts on aging*

- *Nostalgic, graphic look-backs on past pop culture themes and events*

- *For the grandkids: puzzles and games provided by their partner at Highlights™ for Children*

- PS Magazine also is proud to offer custom publishing opportunities and private-label print/digital issues to its Partner Communities.

- PS Enrichment brings diverse and engaging programming, ranging from salon and spa parties to book tours and interactive musical performances. To date, PS Enrichment has organized hundreds of special events in collaboration with Life Enrichment and Activities Directors.

The four overarching topic areas for amenities and the Residential Experience are: Health and Wellness, Education and Mental Stimulation, Entertainment, and Social Activities, which we will examine in turn. As you'll see from the following list, your imagination and your community's unique circumstances are the only limits on the size and scope of activities you choose. If you need a little more motivation, consider getting a copy of *The Big Book of Senior Living Activities* by Debbie Bera and Jillian Thomas. The book features more than 100 activities communities can use to offer a welcoming environment and ensure an active, social community. It covers activities for residents with unique needs, detailed case studies on senior living activities and tips to gain resident and staff buy-in.

HEALTH AND WELLNESS

Interactivity, both physical and mental, helps seniors maintain their independence, enhance their wellbeing, maintain mental and emotional vitality, and help them enjoy a better quality of life. Keeping seniors mentally, physically, emotionally, and socially engaged helps them enjoy a higher quality of life, retain better cognitive function, stay healthier, and live independently longer.

Communities that support and enhance both physical and

cognitive fitness that extend longevity and enhance residents' overall quality of life will be in high demand.

At no other time in our history has there been a greater focus on seniors staying active and healthy. The number of people aged 60 and above who report exercising for at least 30 minutes per day reached 37% in 2014 and will likely continue to steadily increase. Support for promoting exercise in seniors and the positive benefits of such are well documented.

Exercise makes seniors stronger and less likely to fall according to the National Center for Injury Prevention and Control. As an interesting side note, emotional and physical well being apparently tie together. The Australian National University Centre for Mental Health Research found that those in a 787-member study group who scored higher in emotional well being were less likely to fall. The risk rose for those who experienced increased depressive symptoms or lower morale as the study progressed.
A study by the Washington University School of Medicine reported in The Annals of Behavioral Medicine that seniors who exercised scored higher on an emotional health scale. And even though nearly 65 percent of the study's 1,733 participants had arthritis, overall they reported no increase in pain from the exercise.

A British Medical Journal found that exercise is more effective than home hazard modifications and vision correction in preventing seniors' at-home falls.

Exercise helps reduce the severity of illness. A study from Denmark published in Neurology magazine reports that stroke patients who were the most physically active before their illnesses were two and a half times more likely to have a less severe stroke than the least active patients and a better chance for long-term recovery.

Researchers at the University of Illinois at Urbana-Champaign reported that seniors who are physically active in leisure, occupational or home activities such as housecleaning or gardening, report a greater feeling of self-esteem and quality of life.

Considering the robust research supporting exercise, senior living communities should draft a physical activity strategy. Plus, the number of seniors with varying fitness levels demands a comprehensive and diversified program outside the basic "exercise room."

From a community standpoint, healing gardens, therapy pools, aquatic centers or putting greens may be key differentiators in choosing a community. Senior living facilities will be challenged to include diverse offerings of activities and community experience.

Classes offer an opportunity to maintain physical fitness and encourage social engagement. Group classes in yoga, Pilates, Tai Chi, strength training, and water aerobics are all popular choices, as are those tailored to specific health conditions. More advanced classes or equipment could also be explored for those interested in maintaining a higher level of fitness. After all, the oldest person to complete a Hawaii Ironman competition was Madonna Buder, a 75-year-old nun from Spokane, Washington.

While not considered exercise per se, dancing combines physical and social activity. The National Heart, Lung and Blood Institute reports that dancing can lower blood pressure, strengthen bones, lower risk of heart disease, and help manage weight. As a social activity dancing also stimulates the mind and reduces the risk of dementia according to a study in the New England Journal of Medicine.

For expanded opportunities off campus, transportation to swimming facilities, spas, golf courses, and tennis courts is in order.

Wellness, of course, extends beyond what we "do" with our bodies to what we put "in" them. Gardening can be an active component of an overall healthy eating philosophy. A resident's garden allows seniors to plant and harvest produce that may be sold onsite or in local farmer's markets providing a perfect combination of activity, community involvement, and personal fulfillment.

EDUCATION AND MENTAL STIMULATION

Mental stimulation ensures minds are active, contributing to better mental and emotional functioning.

A study in the New England Journal of Medicine found that elderly people who did crossword puzzles four times a week had a risk of dementia 47% lower than those who did the puzzles once a week.

The Memory and Aging Project at Rush University Medical Center published a study in Neurology, the journal of the American

Academy of Neurology that found that a cognitively active senior was 2.6 times less likely to develop dementia than a cognitively inactive senior.

The fusion of technology with lifelong learning results in innovative solutions that promote connectivity to each other and the surrounding community.

Within the context of educational pursuits, residents may find themselves in a position to both take classes and/or give classes, or simply to enjoy demonstrations by local experts in the community. Ongoing opportunities for enthusiastic Instruction & Education as well as Demonstrative Activities, are substantial at any number of levels.

Consider the following:

- Foreign Languages

- Music and Instruments

- 2-D Arts/Crafts – painting, photography

- 3-D Art/Crafts – sculpting, macramé, ceramics

- Technology

- Gardening

- Cooking and Baking

- Writing – Journaling, Poetry, Recording personal histories
- Storytelling

- Reading, Books on Tape and Book Clubs

- Tutoring and Mentoring

- Other Special Interest Groups

Oak Hammock, a retirement community located in Gainesville, Florida, holds a truly unique partnership with nearby

University of Florida (UF). The community's Institute for Learning In Retirement (ILR) has become a model for successful educational programming, largely due to the support of former UF President John Lombardi and other faculty.

All residents of North Florida, aged 55 and older, may participate in the ILR. What started with just 70 students from the surrounding community has grown to more than 250 (including about 60% of Oak Hammock residents) regular participants and approximately 550 members. Modest fees allow the program to grow. Dues for Oak Hammock residents are included in their living fees. Annual fees for those outside Oak Hammock are just $25 with an additional $10 for each course taken.

Six week long courses, taught by volunteer (but professional) teachers cover a wide range of topics. Recent offerings include "Enjoying the Opera" and "Explorations in Geology."

On a more modest front, my inspiration for Tuscan Gardens, my mother, was a lifelong learner. She stayed active to the greatest extent possible until the very end of her life. In addition to being an exceptional cook, she enjoyed arts and crafts such as crochet, macramé, and ceramics. Tuscan Gardens is about hosting multiple classes, like the cooking demonstrations held in the big Tuscan kitchen, inspired by her and her many interests.

In the near future, we expect to launch Tuscan Tours, educational tours for our residents as well as their families. While the cooking classes at the community are fun and fulfilling, imagine how much more meaningful it will be to tour Tuscany with us and take similar classes in la bella Italia.

ENTERTAINMENT

Entertainment can be separated into both onsite and offsite opportunities, including:

- Movies and Theater

- Opera

- Art Museums

- Concerts, Singing and Instrument Recitals

- Visiting Chef Events

- Themed Parties

- Dog Shows

- Car Shows

- Restaurants

- Shopping

I particularly admire what American House, a mid-west senior living system with approximately 40 communities in Michigan and Illinois with a few in Florida, is doing when it comes to music for its residents. American House has partnered with the Detroit Symphony Orchestra, the Grand Rapids Symphony, and the Naples (Florida) Philharmonic to bring live symphonic entertainment to residents, many of whom would not necessarily be able to access this type of experience.

Groups of two or three musicians visit several of the communities – a "tour" you might say – performing for an hour and then participating in a beverage and hors d'oeuvres reception.

Tuscan Gardens aspires to offer equally innovative experiences, musical and otherwise.

SOCIAL ACTIVITIES

Social engagement keeps people connected with friends and involved in events and interests.

A study published in the British Medical Journal involving more than 2,700 seniors showed that social and productive activities like gardening, shopping and preparing meals, were just as beneficial to the subjects' health and quality of life as physical fitness activities. It also indicated that the less physically active a senior was, the greater the health benefit reaped from being socially engaged.

A Harvard School of Public Health study reported in the American Journal of Public Health that the most socially active seniors had the slowest rate of memory decline from over a six-year period. Memory loss among the most socially engaged seniors was less than half that of the least engaged.

Today's senior expects much more than a weekly bingo game, social activities run the gamut from clubs and meetings in any topic area you might consider to:

- Happy Hour and Wine Tastings

- Cards and Games

- Walking and Activity Groups

- Wii Videogames

- Dance

Family friendly environments will become increasingly important to the senior of today and tomorrow. Knowing that their choice of community accommodates guests, both children and grandchildren will become a deciding factor for many retirees.

Certainly our environments must recognize and support the aging bodies and weakening senses of our residents, but it must also be engaging enough to stimulate families. Families, that is sons, daughters, grandsons and granddaughters, visit residences that feel comfortable and fun for themselves, too.

In the past, the primary concern for a senior entering a senior living community was security. This concern has been rapidly replaced with the comfort and design of the living unit, the quality and quantity of dining programs/venues, and the selection of activities and wellness programs.

Today's seniors prefer communities with multiple "restaurant-worthy" dining venues, open display kitchens that allow interaction with the chefs, and an atmosphere that is conducive and welcoming to several generations in the family.

If once there, children and grandchildren can access high-end spa and salon services such as massages and facials, as well as sophisticated fitness programs and equipment, the extended family will return time and time again. And, that boosts resident satisfaction in immeasurable ways.

THE "MEMORY CARE" RESIDENT EXPERIENCE

This chapter would not be complete without a reference to the Resident Experience as it pertains to Memory Care. Like any other resident, Memory Care residents deserve to have stimulating experiences, too. Jolene Brackey's book, *Creating Moments of Joy Along the Alzheimer's Journey,* covers experiential topics like outings, holidays, arts and crafts, and more. It offers a wonderful perspective on enhancing the lives of dementia residents through a series of meaningful "moments," rather than days.

HIGHLIGHTS

1. The Senior Living industry finds itself in an enviable position of having an ever-widening target market, but also a challenging position of having to accommodate hugely varying needs across a vast age spectrum, from 65 to centenarians and everything in between.

2. Experience design is the way of the future in senior living. It elevates simple products and services to memorable moments with the accompanying higher price tag. Evaluate potential offerings through an experiential lens.

3. Yesterday's hospitality model has given way to a concierge model, which consciously aligns around an elevated experience in every area: architecturally, interior design, programmatically, food, activities, and enrichment.

4. Consulting organizations can assist with designing an enriching portfolio of programming.

5. Interactivity, both physical and mental, helps seniors maintain their independence, enhances their well-being, maintains mental and emotional vitality, and helps them enjoy a better quality of life.

6. Communities that welcome and accommodate all generations lead to greater satisfaction among residents. In the past the primary concern for a senior entering a senior living community

was security. This concern has been rapidly replaced with the comfort and design of the living unit, the quality and quantity of dining programs/venues, and the selection of activities and wellness programs.

CHAPTER 10

INTEGRATING TECHNOLOGY

Technology is nothing. What's important is that you have a faith in people, that they're basically good and smart, and if you give them tools, they'll do wonderful things with them.
~ Steve Jobs

Technology plays a key role in today's senior living environment – even before a resident sets foot in a community to make it his or her home. That's because the prospective resident likely used technology to make their senior living decision in the first place, both from the standpoint of informative articles about the wisdom of making the transition and also vetting specific communities.

We truly live in a time when more information is available on any conceivable topic than any other time in history. Today's senior is also becoming surprisingly technologically savvy. Even for those of an extreme old age who are less comfortable with or potentially physically and psychologically distanced from gadgets, family members probably researched and reviewed potential communities on the senior's behalf before approaching any community about possible residency.

This greater access to information via the Internet allows your potential resident to conduct a more thorough and comprehensive evaluation of available community choices.

While word of mouth is still an exceptional method of advertising for senior living communities and plays a significant role in the choice of a community, having a robust web presence with a highly interactive and engaging site ensures that a community can make a resident's "short list" of places to review. Expanding

151

the breadth and depth of your Internet presence can maximize your "connection" with potential residents, as will a strategic use of social media targeted to older Americans.

As a matter of fact, 149 senior living marketing executives surveyed by Brooks Adams Research and the American Seniors Housing Association (ASHA) ranked community websites as the most effective way to market senior communities at 68%, followed by direct mail (51%), education, and then in-person social events (38%).

Once happily ensconced in a meaningful residential living environment, technology can serve several purposes for seniors to enhance *The Art of Living.* Therefore, the community that provides both tools and training will reap the benefits of a vibrant population who will use that connectivity to access news, information, government services, health resources and opportunities for social support as well as to share their positive experiences with potential new residents.

While it's estimated that only 20% of the population over age 85 will be able to readily adopt technology, according to Dr. David Rhew, Chief Medical Officer for Samsung, he does see an opportunity to make some headway, getting them more engaged and achieving some things previously thought impossible.

Some communities use service providers like Connected Living. Through a powerful combination of cloud and mobile technology, lifelong learning content and highly skilled engagement consulting, Connected Living connects communities, home, and mobile health to revolutionize the aging experience. Their user-friendly technology suite increases community staff efficiency and improves residents' ability to interact with each other, their family members, and the world.

Connected Living is a social impact company founded to bridge the "digital divide" for the 17 million seniors in the United States who have been left out of the daily conversation. Being connected provides older adults with a voice and ability to make a positive social impact on all generations. Connected Living believes strongly in providing transformational technologies that allow people to connect, contribute and lead healthier lives.

Connected Living has discovered that seniors will adopt technology more readily when they can connect with family and friends, receive engaging content and access high-touch support.

The Connected Living team sees the impact everyday, knows that seniors will connect, and when they do it has a completely transformative impact on their happiness, engagement, and health.

The Connected Living web-based offering has:

- Connected over 60,000 older adults residing in senior living communities across the United States, to their families and friends.

- Served the largest private senior living providers, public and affordable housing properties, PACE programs, veterans groups, and health care organizations across the nation.

- Proven the impact that mobile devices have when they are put in the hands of seniors proving that "A Connected Life is a Healthier Life."

Connected Living offers the following programs:

- **Connected Living Network - Administrator Dashboard:** The powerful web-based content management system centralizes input and management of communication, content, surveys, calendars, and data for Corporate and Community Administrators. Content entered into the Connected Living Network flows seamlessly from the CLN Administrator Dashboard to the Resident & Family Panel, Digital Signage, and its mobile app.

  The Connected Living Network is a HIPAA compliant community social network that provides residents and associates with a wealthy inventory of enrichment curricula and engagement programming. It gives family members new ways to digitally interact with residents and a window into the daily life of a community.

- **Digital Signage & In-House TV:** Connected Living has partnered with Four Winds Interactive to create the state-of-the-art digital signage solution for Senior Living providers. Through a simple consultative process, the in-house design team creates stunning branded displays that engage residents and make a lasting impression on Community prospects and visitors.

- **The Connected Living Mobile App:** The Connected Living app allows users to share important information, daily, through an internal social network, GPS functionality and activity sensors so everyone can experience enhanced "peace of mind" knowing those they care most about are OK.

Any senior living community should give careful consideration to supporting technologically savvy seniors (generally the younger or more affluent type who are adept at using technology and online platforms) as well as getting those less comfortable and/or disconnected (usually older or less affluent seniors) up to speed on the advantages that digital tools and services provide.

A couple ways you can encourage adoption of technology include hosting demonstrations for how to use different devices or apps or providing devices to residents as part of a move-in package with certain apps pre-loaded.

Supporting the technologically advanced requires a full Wi-Fi enabled premises and access to tablets and or smart TVs. Training the less technologically adept may mean instructor-led classes conducted in a well-equipped computer "lab" of sorts. The relative emphasis placed on each would be discovered by assessing the skill level and needs of any particular resident population.

With respect to the private technological experience of residents at Tuscan Gardens, enabling wireless technology within each private living quarter along with a computer for them to access maintains a sense of connectivity throughout their day. Ideally, the computer is a "keyboard-less" system that operates 100% on touch, yet has full system capability.

Large icons on the home screen drive the functionality. Hungry for something sweet from the kitchen? Tap the wooden spoon icon, view the menu and place an online order. Excited to tell your son that you signed up for piano lessons? Touch the phone icon, view the phone directory and tap the photo of your son to instantly dial. Integrated video chat technology lets you see him as you speak.

At Tuscan Gardens, the computer is intended to come with a personal website for each resident, allowing individuals the opportunity to incorporate all of life's memories into a unique digital record that belongs entirely to the resident. Residents can upload photographs, stories, and scanned memorabilia from their lives into a unique and personalized website that can be an ongoing activity that is eventually bequeathed to family members.

ASSISTIVE TECHNOLOGIES

Several components of the foregoing could be considered assistive technology, devices that aid people in performing day to day functions. A wheelchair, walker or cane by itself could be defined as such. However, true assistive technology (emphasis on the word *technology*) is becoming more sophisticated every day. While much of what follows is available for both aging in place or senior living communities, many may be price prohibitive for the average senior or community. Regardless, technological choices must be acceptable to the senior and not seen as an intrusion. Budget notwithstanding, options should fit the person rather than the person fitting the option.

Personal emergency response systems (PERS) nearly became an object of ridicule with the now infamous television commercial that proclaimed, "I've fallen and I can't get up." At the time of the aforementioned advertisement, a typical PERS featured a type of device worn around the neck with a button pushed by a senior to summon help. As straightforward and low-tech as this item might seem, it still had its drawbacks in that it wasn't effective for people who could be forgetful or so severely incapacitated that even a button-push was an impossibility. Beyond that, some seniors were simply too embarrassed to summon help in this way.

Enter today's PERS devices that nearly remove the human equation. Technology has progressed to the point that PERS will automatically signal for help. The intuitive devices can differentiate between a real "fall" and a senior simply bending over to pick up a dropped item. They still tend to be worn around the neck for convenience sake and require a monthly fee.

Great Call and Philips Lifeline are two popular and highly rated PERS devices.

- **Philips Lifeline:** A leader in fall detection and a national provider. The basic **HomeSafe** system is a speakerphone for communicating with emergency services and a waterproof help button to call for help that can be worn as a pendant or wristband. Stepping up to **HomeSafe with AutoAlert** provides a waterproof pendant capable of detecting falls and automatically calling for help if the pendant senses no motion for 30 seconds. For both HomeSafe options, the help button has a long life battery and the speakerphone has a backup battery that lasts for up to 30 hours in case of a power outage. So they won't have to worry about charging a device. Both require a monthly fee.

- **GreatCall 5Star Urgent Response:** For active seniors on-the-go, GreatCall offers an affordable PERS solution that uses its 5Star Urgent Response system cellular network. The **GreatCall Splash** device provides a wireless call-button that connects the wearer directly to a GreatCall emergency response agent or 911.

  An upgraded package provides seniors with an Urgent Care line staffed with registered nurses and board-certified doctors. Caregivers receive status updates of calls or incidents. Fall detection is available for an added fee. This automatically calls the Urgent Response line when the device detects a fall. All require a monthly fee.

The ability to take prescribed medicine on time and in the proper amount is a significant milestone in determining whether a person is able to continue to live independently or would be better served in a higher assistance level community. Studies show that 20% to 30% of people who end up in skilled nursing facilities make the transition simply because they can't manage medication on their own.

In order to assist seniors with this task, manufacturers are marketing medication management tools. One countertop-style model is about the size of a small appliance. In using this device, a caregiver adds several days' worth of medication into the unit and then provides the dispenser's manufacturer with the patient's medication schedule. The manufacturer programs the machine to deliver the appropriate amount of medication at the proper time.

Obviously, this tool requires some human intervention – the use of a professional caregiver on at least a weekly basis. It also requires an installation fee and monthly rental fee for the machine and monitoring fees for the medication.

Depending on the type of medication management device chosen, some can be locked to prevent the taking of wrong medicine or extra doses by someone who is in the early stages of dementia or simply a little forgetful. Others can notify a caregiver or administrator by phone, email or text if a dosage is missed.

Current medication management systems on the market include TabSafe and MedCoach.

- **TabSafe:** TabSafe is an easy-to-use, effective solution for managing medications yet can accommodate even the most complex schedules. The medication management system reminds the user, dispenses medications, alerts caregivers before a dose time is missed, and monitors adherence. TabSafe improves medication adherence to over 96%, leading to better health outcomes and avoids preventable costly emergency visits and hospitalizations. The security features and online reporting provide peace-of-mind for users and their caregivers.

- **MedCoach:** The MedCoach Medication Reminder app provides daily pill medication reminders and automatic refills.

Motion detecting devices aka motion sensors can assist offsite caregivers in determining whether a senior's normal day to day activities appear disrupted. Leveraging wires within floor mats or bed mats caregivers can be alerted to changes in usual patterns or unexpected events like the front door opening.

These devices require someone to program in an individual's baseline activity such as when the person usually gets up and dressed and goes to the kitchen for breakfast. In that way, it's able to detect anomalies in the patterns. The costs for the sensors and the ongoing monitoring can be cost prohibitive for many private citizens.

As the technology progresses, look for motion sensor programs that offer greater remote functionality and integration with video cameras, door locks, thermostats, and lights, as well as lower costs when controlled by free apps that require no monthly fees.

Enhanced telephones assist seniors with vision reduction, hearing loss or cognitive impairment. Oversized buttons, amplified sound, and space for photo displays of frequently called people on speed dial keep residents independent.

Some CCRCs have taken the leap to actually testing "smart apartments." The Masons of California, operators of three CCRCs, retrofitted apartments in two Independent Living communities to see what tech was actually helpful and what might be considered "tech for tech's sake." The adjustments included voice controls, motion sensors, and medication dispensers.

The "tech" actually being used at The Masons of California doesn't even come close to the tech imagined by the student exhibition winners of the 2016 Senior Housing News Design awards. The winning team, made up of graduate students at The University of Kansas (KU) presented a technologically advanced redesign of a current KU faculty retirement location, Sprague Hall. Some of the technology incorporated by the team included gait-analysis floor sensors, hydration monitoring smart toilets, sensor-integrated beds for evaluating sleep patterns and medicine dispensers that sort pills.

No matter what type of assistive technologies are chosen for an individual senior or an entire community, proper training is the key to habitual use. Assistive technology serves no purpose if it's disregarded after installation as simply too technical, too confusing or too much trouble.

Technologies based in communities have the advantage of the ability to schedule and host training sessions to ensure users understand the product's features and functionality. A "help desk" of sorts can be a worthwhile endeavor – even if it's only staffed a few hours a day – to move users through the learning curve and into common usage.

Getting seniors accustomed to these assistive tools requires buy-in. If they understand what the product is and what it can do for them, they are more likely to work through the aches and pains of adopting the technology. If the item seems to ask too much of them for too little payoff, it's simply going to be a "marketing brochure" brag –something that sounds great in theory, but never gets practiced.

COMMUNITY TECHNOLOGY

The technologies necessary to improve daily life from a personal or consumer standpoint seem to be light years ahead from the community aspect of technology. It seems to be the one area that is stagnant. Solutions at the provider level, operational level, and regulatory level are stuck two decades behind.

Consider the revolutionary Amazon Echo (aka Alexa). What appears to be simply a black cylinder with an integrated audio system is virtually an invisible personal assistant. Perpetually connected to the cloud via wifi, Echo interacts with users by voice. It listens continually through various microphones placed throughout the room and understands questions and commands, all prefaced by it's first name "Alexa."

Echo's applications include streaming music, searching online, or playing audiobooks. It can even read your kindle to you. Check the calendar, traffic and weather with Echo. Book an Uber or ask for recipes that contain the four things you have left in the fridge.

When you consider all the amazing things Echo is capable of, and the incredible applications it has for senior living, you'll find it particularly quaint at how far behind the regulatory bodies are in updating compliance code. With the sorts of sophisticated motion detectors, sound activation and virtual assistants like Echo, regulatory bodies still require senior living communities be equipped with pull cords.

Yes, you read that right. I could design every suite in Tuscan Gardens with full motion detection in every room to capture in real time whether a fall has taken place, but I can't obtain an occupational license without a pull cord in the bathroom. So, a senior can fall anywhere else, or even fall in the bathroom with no ability to get to the pull cord, but somehow this is preferable for the regulators to a technologically advanced system.

I call it "institutional lethargy." It's a very slow process at every level. It's particularly frustrating when considering the software platforms that run a senior living community. Technological providers have still not integrated their platforms. One may have strong marketing, another strong accounting, and a final one with strong clinical, but I've yet to find an integrated model that sings, or that is fully accessible with smart technology.

For wellness, most people consider Yardi clinical to be top

notch. However, Eldercare may be best for pure senior living as opposed to CCRC or property management.

What I'm describing here is what I defined years ago as a unified business platform (UBP). It's a common communications platform that spans the length and breadth, from head to toe, of a company's skeletal structure, into every square of its organizational chart. And like the nervous system of the human body, it provides a means of instant, enterprise-wide, multi-dimensional communication.

In a more traditional business model, sales figures can be read and analyzed by management. The sales force dealing with clientele in the field can interface with engineers in R&D who are designing products for that clientele. Accounting can track expenditures throughout the company — and pinpoint areas for reducing costs. The UBP is the ultimate system for letting the left hand know what the right hand is doing.

By way of background, as the business community moved into the age of information technologies, thousands of software platforms were developed and sold to meet every need of every function of an organization.

I can illustrate this proliferation of independently designed software systems with a classic story from early railroading. Two railroad companies agreed to build a single railroad system across 19th-century America, to connect the East with the pioneer West. When the two tracks met, somewhere in the Great Plains, it was discovered that they had laid their tracks using two different gauges of rail.

More than a century later, as computers came of age in virtually every major corporation, the accounting department bought accounting software, human resources installed HR software, sales and marketing and management, and every branch office and assembly plant bought its own software — and none of it was compatible. Many corporations today operate the same way: each department happily processing data on a legacy software platform unable to communicate with other software, or any newer, more sophisticated software other departments maybe using.

Suppose our human bodies were constructed the same way — as if each arm, each leg, our brain and heart had their own nervous systems. You might cut your finger and bleed to death while your arm was still trying to communicate pain to your head. A bee landing on your nose would sting you before your hand got the message to swat it away.

The key term is "unified," in that a unified business platform carries the data in real time to all areas of the organism simultaneously. For an entrepreneur running a small consumer-goods business with no associates, he or she is the unified business platform. But for every new partner and associate that comes on board, that UBP must expand as surely as new phones and computer terminals.

Companies have different types of UBPs, but they all have the same purpose: to gather information and intelligence, both within and beyond the walls of the organization.

At my former company, we created a unified business platform we called eVoyager, written in-house to meet our specific requirements. It took us months and was no easy task, but we ended up with a UBP that served us regardless of how we expanded or grew. (By the way, eVoyager was named after the Voyager 1 satellite featured in *StarTrek 2*.)

We had originally bought a system from a company called iMIS to carry data on sales and marketing in the mid-nineties. The iMIS System was pitched to us as an "integrated database." As it turned out, regardless of what the software publisher claimed, the system was not even remotely integrated. It was, at best, an event planning tool, and a not particularly good sales and marketing program. When we brought some technology in-house, we took a look at iMIS and asked ourselves a fundamental question: Would this system enable us to run all aspects of the company — from the external environment to internal accounting and processing, shipping, back office accounting, finance administration, and profit-and-loss, as well as all the monitoring and metrics that were necessary for us to understand how well we were actually operating?

After six months of study of all of our different software systems we had in the company, the answer was no. At the time we began that process we were generating about $8.5 million in sales with 50 associates. So we decided to build a system that would be fully integrated and would represent a complete and unified business platform for the entire company. By the way, "unified business platform" was not a common term at the time, or even a particularly common term now. There were "CRM applications," "enterprise solutions," and various other terms, but the term "unified business platform" was or is not commonly bandied about.

So we began the process of building an original UBP. We worked backward to create the system. We started by identifying the most basic requirements, by asking ourselves, "What do we need to know?" — *i.e.*, absolutely critical information. We then identified the metrics we needed to obtain that information, and do it in real time. We then produced hard copy, on plain paper, in order to get this information literally in people's hands at any particular time, whether it's daily, weekly, monthly or in real time as needed.

We had to capture the information in order to manipulate it in the way we wanted. We had to make sure the information was tied together uniformly and that we had all the different types of legacy data incorporated into it. We then had to begin producing reports on an automated basis. We knew that our managers needed to access their information as easily as possible, so we made sure that it was systemized in a way that was flexible enough for individuals who didn't have a strong technology background to pull the reports.

Eventually, we were able to incorporate all legacy systems into eVoyager and it performed brilliantly, giving us the intrinsic communication we needed to run every aspect of our organization from top to bottom, vertically and horizontal — all the way from external customers to sales and marketing to human resources to back-office accounting to purchase orders to project management.

The point of this discussion is that the senior living industry is crying out for a UBP exactly like that. Any number of companies out there who really understand the need to address technology in a senior living scenario will likely find a great deal of communities clamoring for the product they eventually create.

LOOKING TOWARD TOMORROW

Technology needs of the residents shouldn't overshadow the technology needs of the staff. Moving toward a paperless environment means professional staff discards clipboards in favor of handheld technology (tablets or smartphones, for example). Connecting these devices to a single primary program for the community allows any notes or photos taken to be centralized.

Data-driven procurement systems and computerized menu planning software keep your community fiscally responsible and time efficient.

A system of cameras permits a password-protected live feed from the common areas so that loved ones can see what's happening at Tuscan Gardens at any time. The individual may or may not see Mom or Dad passing by at a given time of the day – that's what the in-room video chat capability is for – they will be assured that "living well" is taking place in the dining rooms, conversation nooks or activities rooms. That level of technology and type of privileged access provides for a level of quality control that is exceptional at every level.

In closing, I'm reminded of a testy exchange I had early in 2010 with a caregiver at a senior living conference. This individual had remarked that she would never consider working at a "facility" that used "nanny cams." I was horrified and immediately retorted that I would never consider hiring a caregiver who was not prepared to work in an environment that recorded everything that was happening all of the time. Needless to say, the conversation did not end well.

HIGHLIGHTS

1. Today's senior is incredibly technologically savvy and very likely to use technology to make their senior living decision in the first place, both from the standpoint of informative articles about the wisdom of making the transition and also vetting specific communities.

2. This greater access to information via the Internet allows your potential resident to conduct a more thorough and comprehensive evaluation of available community choices. Ensure that your website is robust, highly interactive, and engaging.

3. Encourage adoption of technology by hosting demonstrations for how to use different devices or apps or providing devices to residents as part of a move-in package with certain apps pre-loaded.

4. Assistive technology is any device that aids people in performing day to day functions.

5. New sophisticated assistive technology includes personal emergency response systems and medication reminders.

6. Technology should be woven seamlessly throughout the community and lead to enhanced lives rather than "tech for tech's sake."

CHAPTER 11

THOUGHTS ON MEMORY CARE

Those with dementia are still people and they still have stories and they still have character and they're all individuals and they're all unique. And they just need to be interacted with on a human level.
~ Carey Mulligan

While this book is not a clinical volume, but rather a treatise on *The Art of Living* at whatever age or stage of life, it seems appropriate that we discuss dementia and its impact on the seniors who are our current or potential customers.

The statistics are nothing short of alarming. Of the 79 million total Baby Boomers who are retired or retiring in the coming years, approximately 28 million are expected to develop some sort of dementia of which Alzheimer's is the most common form. Interestingly, women are more likely than men to suffer dementia, but this could be simply because they have the longer life span. A 65-year-old woman has a 17% chance of developing some form of dementia; a man of the same age just 9%. Those who beat the lifespan odds (of either gender) and reach the age of 85 increase their chances to even money – 50-50. One in three seniors dies with some form of dementia, but it's not an instant death sentence. Some people can live with dementia for up to 30 years.

While people are most familiar with Alzheimer's disease, more than 100 types of dementia are documented. As of the time of this publishing, more than 5.5 million Americans are living with Alzheimer's. That's about 70 percent of people with dementia. The number is expected to triple within the next few decades.

Yet, great strides are being made around the world in this

challenging field of health care. For example, Dementia Villages are redefining what it means to live with dementia. Begun in the Netherlands, Hogeweyk is a specially designed gated village with 23 houses for 152 dementia-suffering seniors. The residents live in houses differentiated by seven different lifestyles formed around mutual interests: upper class, homey, Christian, artisan, Indonesian, and cultural. The residents manage their own households together with a constant team of staff members trained to work with dementia patients. Daily household chores are done in all of the houses. Groceries are purchased in the village supermarket.

The ultimate in private and autonomous living, the village boasts streets, squares, gardens and a park where the residents can safely roam free. The village offers amenities like a restaurant, a bar, and a theatre. Village residents decline up to five times more slowly, without medication, as compared to the average.

Not to be outdone by our European cousins, Ohio-based The Lantern Group has recently opened the doors on its Lantern of Chagrin Valley, an assisted living and memory care community that resembles a circa-1930s or 1940s village. A large indoor courtyard with grass colored carpet, lampposts, and fountains are home to memory care units designed to resemble a small home with its own front porch. The most remarkable feature is the fiberoptic ceiling that simulates the natural sky, allowing for sunrises and sunsets, as well as meandering clouds.

The intent, according to Lantern Group founder and CEO Jean Makash is to remind residents of their younger years. Coupled with music therapy and aromatics, Makesh hopes to stimulate residents' senses, increase neural networks and enhance their ability to live more independently.

While the development of communities like these is encouraging, all dementia sufferers, no matter their residential situation deserve the best conditions for a quality of life.

The Alzheimer's Disease Bill of Rights developed by Virginia Bell and David Troxel is designed to help dementia sufferers develop a sense of independence, exercise their right to be informed of their condition, and leverage opportunities for engagement.

Every person diagnosed with Alzheimer's disease or a related disorder deserves:

- **To be informed of one's diagnosis.**

- **To have appropriate, ongoing medical care.**

- **To be productive in work and play as long as possible.**

- **To be treated like an adult, not a child.**

- **To have expressed feelings taken seriously.**

- **To be free from psychotropic medications if at all possible.**

- **To live in a safe, structured and predictable environment.**

- **To enjoy meaningful activities to fill each day.**

- **To be out-of-doors on a regular basis.**

- **To have physical contact including hugging, caressing, and hand-holding.**

- **To be with persons who know one's life story, including cultural and religious traditions.**

- **To be cared for by individuals well-trained in dementia care.**

A BRIEF DISCUSSION ON DEMENTIA

Note: my comments are not intended to be a clinical exposition on the subject, but rather a casual overview of dementia and how it impacts individuals. A great deal of this information comes to me from my good friend Joshua Freitas. Joshua is on the cutting edge of dementia care programming. He holds five certifications related to dementia care and has studied at some of the world's most renowned colleges and universities, including Lesley University, Harvard University and Berklee College of Music. I highly recommend Joshua's book, *The Dementia Concept*, for a comprehensive understanding of the various forms of dementia and a discussion of some of the most successful dementia programming practiced today.

Throughout our life we perceive and process information to navigate the world. This perceiving and processing leads to two different types of knowledge. Propositional knowledge is the type of knowledge developed through life experiences. It has a lot to do with past memories and events. It dictates our understanding of cultural rules and cues. Sensory knowledge is gathered through the senses. It's based largely on the present environment, the "here and now" you might call it.

Because dementia affects propositional knowledge, sensory knowledge becomes a much more important way to navigate the world. In fact, people in early stages of dementia continue to depend on proposition knowledge about their backgrounds, likes, dislikes, values, and habits. As the disease progresses this type of propositional or "unconscious" knowledge fades due to a decrease in neural activity and sensory or "gut feeling" type knowledge replaces it.

Contrary to what many people believe, dementia doesn't signal the end of learning. It's just a different type of learning to help people live in the best way possible. They have a capacity to create new memories and develop new skills with the right support and guidance, which can lead to increasing individual levels of success.

Not all dementia treatments involve pharmacological interventions. Many programs emphasize expressive arts therapy, music therapy, social engagement, and exercise as holistic treatment that considers mental and social factors. Taken together this type of holistic treatment can increase physical functionality, fine motor skills and even eyesight.

The key improvement for dementia patients, however, is improvement in plasticity. Plasticity is the brain's ability to detour around its injured parts to find new ways to perform lost skills. Improved plasticity helps dementia patients reroute the synaptic network of information processing. Parts of the brain can grow and strengthen, very much like any other muscle, when they are used and challenged continuously. By encouraging, supporting, and empowering dementia patients with learning opportunities, you can help them overcome challenges on their own.

People with dementia can learn in several different ways, but all will generally require more time than learning opportunities for non-dementia sufferers. Allow plenty of time to attempt new tasks and don't step in even if struggling occurs. Empower them to try, not to rely on you. Performing tasks for dementia patients hastens their loss of self-sufficiency. Struggling serves a beneficial purpose in that it reinforces skills and creates memories of pathways used to approach challenges. Viewing a dementia patient has helpless fosters forgetfulness and physical inhibition and sets the stage for the disease to progress faster.

Contrary to the belief that favors repetitive brain games, the best brain activities require patients to consistently perform new tasks. Repetition improves success at completing a single task. A variety of new tasks helps form multiple skills.

Embedding new skills with new routines reaches the highest rate of brain stimulation. However, new skills take time to develop, approximately 35 days for a dementia patient. Providing reminders when practicing skills helps form new routines. Reinforcing success with praise and rewards can motivate a patient to leave their comfort zone and overcome challenges.

Routines empower successful outcomes and successful outcomes encourage participation. Routines make daily activities familiar and increase the chances they are performed well. Active and engaged seniors enjoy increased mental health and happiness and sustain life skills for a longer period of time.

Caregivers can use cues or hints when assisting with tasks to lessen agitation and set the stage for success. Perhaps the greatest role caregivers can play during these learning opportunities is as cheerleader. A positive tone of voice and encouraging words are invaluable.

Following are different types of learning, some of which promote neuroplasticity:

- *Procedural learning* focuses on repetition to develop new habits. Procedural learning requires equal parts of information and support. Offer the right amount of instruction and be available for assistance to increase their success and reduce confusion. Let the person do as much as possible before offering clues or help.

- *Physical learning*, as the name implies, emphasizes a physical action. It can refer to actual exercise like walking or stretching or behavioral tasks like those required for daily self-care. The physical nature of physical learning can increase blood flow and promote more neural activity. By repeating a physical activity, muscle memory is reinforced for the dementia patient making tasks easier to perform over the long term. Exercise in general boasts several benefits such as stabilizing mood, alleviating agitation, increasing dexterity, and improving sociability, concentration, and cognitive function. It combats depression, which affects approximately half of dementia sufferers. Physical activity releases endorphins which reduce pain (particularly arthritis pain which affect 60% to 80% of people over age 65) and increase feelings of happiness.

- *Experiential learning* involves new experiences like going to an art gallery or visiting the mall. New experiences focus attention which physically challenges the brain. Experiential learning promotes social participation and provides multi-sensory stimulation, helping the dementia patient create and maintain new memories.

- *Novelty learning* is a fancy way of saying learning new things. This creates new neural brain pathways, which can circumvent injured areas. Learning skills like typing, cooking or foreign language fluency are great examples of novelty learning.

- *Emotional learning* occurs during momentous times in our lives such as births, deaths, weddings, and graduations. These events are filtered through the amygdala which processes sensory experiences and emotions.

Regardless of the type of learning dementia patients embark upon, they are capable of learning and adapting to change. As certain skills are lost, others can become strengthened to compensate. They key is to pique their curiosity and keep them engaged with society and their surroundings.

TYPES OF DEMENTIA

Alzheimer's and vascular dementia are the two most commonly diagnosed forms. Following is a rundown of some of the more common forms and ways that you can work to engage those suffering from those types.

- **Alzheimer's disease** requires caregivers with tremendous patience. Often it's beneficial to move past current times with an Alzheimer's patient and reach into their long-term memory banks. This can be done through photos, books or music from the patient's youth. Family members may be able to provide stories or anecdotes to help with connections. Allow ample time for conversation or directions. Let them take a moment to process the information and respond.

  Art-based expression such as art, dance, poetry writing or music is helpful for individuals who are challenged by communicating verbally. These expressive arts tap into parts of the brain that enrich connections to self and others, allowing patients to cope more easily and feel more at ease.

  Music, in particular, can be a meaningful way to communicate. Consider singing with the patient. It supports and sustains the articulators that allow the physical ability of speech to be maintained.

  Music can promote socialization and lessen challenging behaviors such as sundowning. Sundowning is a psychological phenomenon in which increased confusion and restlessness are experienced at the end of the day and throughout the night.

  Match music to the time of day. Morning time is ideal for upbeat instrumental music. These bright, light melodies set the tone for a good day.

  During the day continue with upbeat, but lesser known music. Keep the music as a pleasant background accent. Familiar music can urge patients to focus on the music and not on the social interaction necessary for them to have a productive day. Less well known music won't distract or overstimulate the listeners, but will increase the sense of ease and enjoyment.

Slower, calming music around sunset tells patients the day is winding down. It enhances performance of quiet, "mindless" tasks that don't require concentration.

- **Vascular Dementia (aka Multi-Infarct Dementia)** is the second most common form of dementia. Vascular dementia patients benefit from mild exercise. Over-exercising leads to confusion. Numbness in the legs may also be an issue. Moving the legs for a minute or two before standing can help with walking and prevent falls.

- **Frontotemporal Dementia** (of which Pick's disease is a type) interferes with the ability to maintain a routine and understand social cues. Keeping a structured schedule and using hand motions when talking can be of great benefit.

- For individuals with **Lewy Body Dementia**, movement can be a key issue. Lifting the feet a minimum of three inches off the ground when walking can help reinforce muscle memory. It can also help to have rhythmic "marching band" type music to assist lifting the feet and walking. Caregivers should support individuals with Lewy Body Dementia on their "dominant hand" side and model moving behaviors like bending at the hip to guide someone to sit. Additionally, negative news can increase hallucinations and delusions in these patients. Monitor the types of programming they listen to or watch.

- **Creutzfeldt-Jakob Disease** can cause argumentativeness or emotional manipulation. Responding with reassurance or validation can diffuse these difficult situations. Interestingly, many Creutzfeldt-Jakob Disease sufferers are motivated to be of assistance. Let them read to fellow residents or perform helpful tasks. Of all forms of dementia, people with this type tend to be most comforted by faith based activities. Be sure they have the opportunity to attend religious services or read inspirational literature.

APPROACHES TO INTERACTION

Dementia patients require engagement just like other residents. Because isolation leads to apathy and depression, engaging with each other and their environment helps dementia patients have an optimal quality of life.

However, as Laura Wayman points out in her excellent book, *A Loving Approach to Dementia Care*, what works for short periods does not work indefinitely. As no two cases are identical, approaches must be tweaked with a live in the moment attitude of gratitude for the good moments that can be had.

Following are a selection of interaction and engagement strategies that senior living team members can leverage with dementia patients.

- *Focus on communicating, whether that's a simple touch on the shoulder or a greeting.* Introduce yourself and provide a "clue" as to who you are. Make eye contact and communicate on the same level, rather than speaking down to the person from above them. If the person seems unhappy, connect on a meaningful level. Show compassion. Match their emotions. Ask what they need and try to provide help. Acknowledge their feelings, but don't allow dark moods to fester. If necessary, direct the conversation to happier, more positive subjects. If available, offer a comfort item to hold.

- *When it's time for activities, offer engaging and varied options.* Invite everyone to participate. Even if they decline, always ask. Allow dementia residents to be involved in choosing their activities, décor, music or staff caregivers if possible. However, when offering choices provide no more than three options.

- *Make sure all activities have a clear beginning and ending.* Sit in a circle or side by side during activities. Be patient and allow plenty of time for activities. Consider the "15" rule of thumb. The average brain tends to process different information every 15 minutes. The average attention span of a person with dementia is 15 minutes. A person with dementia needs 15 minutes to acclimate to the surroundings and another 15 minutes to begin to participate. If anyone in the group begins to exhibit a concerning behavior, give them 15 minutes before redirecting. This allows them to process the information.

• *Appeal to all five senses during activities.* If the activity has a food or aromatic component, offer tastes and/or encourage patients to smell (one of the senses most strongly linked to memory). Allow patients to touch the activity objects. Offer instructions in a loud and clear voice. Use color to stimulate sight.

• *Determine how best to guide patients during activities.* "Hand over hand" places the caregiver in the position of "forcing" the patient. "Hand under hand" allows the individual to rest their hand on yours and feel the process as you perform a task.

• *Connect with each person at the culmination of the activity with a thank you, a hug or a handshake.* This creates an emotional and a physical connection. Express positive and forward-thinking comments when you leave.

• *Offer sincere compliments.* A compliment is simply a recognition of a positive attribute. Compliments encourage positive behavior and increase self esteem and confidence. You can often see physical effects of compliments in a happier mood, brighter smile, and more energetic attitude.

No discussion on interacting with Memory Care residents would be complete without mentioning the Best Friends™ Approach developed in the 1990s by Virginia Bell and David Troxel (cited in the beginning of this chapter for their Alzheimer's Disease Bill of Rights).

Developed while Bell and Troxel worked at the University of Kentucky's Alzheimer's Disease Research Center, the Best Friends™ Approach suggests that what a person suffering from dementia needs most is a "best friend," be that a family member, friend or professional caregiver. A best friend is ideally suited to empathize with the situation, while remaining loving and positive and is dedicated to helping the person feel safe, secure, and valued. The seven building blocks which serve as the foundation for the Best Friends Approach are included below.

BEST FRIENDS APPROACH
SEVEN BUILDING BLOCKS

1. *Recognizing the basic rights of a person with dementia.* Embracing the points in their Dementia Bill of Rights, helps them see and acknowledge the person beneath the cloak of dementia who deserves our best care and support and has the right to live with choice and dignity.

2. *Understanding what it's like to have dementia.* Behaviors seem less strange or unreasonable when you understand that dementia impacts the brain. Understanding what it's like to have dementia helps us develop empathy, become more accepting of the resident and better meet the needs of the person with compassion.

3. *Knowing and using the person's Life Story.* When persons with dementia forget their past, it's up to their Best Friends to do the remembering. Collecting key social and personal history into a form – what we call the Life Story – helps us help the person to recall happy times and successes (a hole-in-one on the golf course or a community award) and gives us tools for redirection when the person is having a bad day (asking a woman who loves to bake to teach you how to make an apple pie).

4. *Knowing just what to say when communication is breaking down.* Dementia damages a person's ability to "make conversation," express their wishes verbally, understand requests or remember directions. Best Friends understand the importance of slowing down and being present for the person with dementia, using good communication skills.

5. *Developing the "knack" of great dementia care.* Knack is the "art of doing difficult things with ease," or "clever tricks and strategies." Acting as a Best Friend, the world view changes. We can practice patience and understanding. If the person says that she likes the president, George Bush, we don't

correct her. Instead, we might say, "I like him too."

6. *Experiencing meaningful engagement throughout the day.* Persons with dementia who no longer can take part in favorite activities or initiate new ones can easily become isolated, bored, and frustrated. Best Friends understand that socialization is therapeutic and can fight depression, keep persons physically fit and foster feelings of happiness and success. Best Friends balance formal activities with unstructured, "in the moment" times that fill our days: taking a short walk, chatting, offering hand massages or doing simple chores together.

7. *Recasting the relationship and your language from staff to Best Friend.* Use the language of friendship throughout your day. When a team meeting is called to discuss a behavior, ask how the staff can be a Best Friend to that resident. Rework job descriptions to emphasize the importance of relationship. During one-on-one time, let the person know that you appreciate the friendship. Using the phrase "Best Friends" and developing authentic relationships ultimately helps the person feel safe, secure, and valued – and creates a caring community where all benefit.

Bell and Troxel's full treatment of this topic is covered in their extraordinary book, *The Best Friends Approach to Dementia Care.*

When selecting a Memory Care community, consider both design and security of the community. Controls should be in place to discourage and prevent wandering without restricting individual freedom, of course. Remember, too, that the progressive nature of various dementias means that a place that meets today's needs may not be appropriate in six months.

I mentioned Lisa Cini and Mosaic Design Studio in "Chapter 6: Interior Spaces." Mosaic has more than 20 years experience designing for memory care communities, helping to create the most nurturing and comfortable environments possible for individuals facing Alzheimer's and dementia, while keeping residents safe and the environment easy to maintain. In closing, I'd like to share some of Lisa's innovations for Memory Care residents – *Nostalgic Nooks/ Lifeskill Stations and Discovery Baskets.*

Nostalgic Nooks/ Lifeskill Stations and Discovery Baskets are meant to echo a joyful or pleasurable time in a Memory Care resident's life. Mosaic offers nine full-size *Nostalgic Nooks/Lifeskill Stations* (gardening, office, kitchen, workbench, nursery, vanity, Snoezelen, Going to the Movies, and Wii Love Life Bowling) and five Discovery Baskets (laundry, sewing, tools, garden, and weddings) intended to suit a wide range of interests and backgrounds.

MEMORY CARE PROGRAMS

Many organizations are doing groundbreaking work in the Memory Care space and I am honored to mention them briefly here.

Inspired Living uses a Positive Approach™ to Memory Care, based on the teaching of renowned expert Teepa Snow. This program focuses on what each person *still can do*, not on the abilities they may have lost.

Clarity Pointe's unique, *Heart*felt CONNECTIONS™ takes a positive, life-affirming approach to memory care, emphasizes capabilities and builds self-confidence, recognizing that what remains is far more important than what has been lost.

In addition to my friend Josh Freitas, whom I quoted before, two other authors I admire are Jennifer Ghent-Fuller and Steven Sabat. Jennifer's works, including *It Isn't Common Sense: Interacting with People Who Have Memory Loss Due to Dementia* and *Thoughtful Dementia Care: Understanding the Dementia Experience*, serve as meaningful guides to navigating this challenging world. Steven's *Alzheimer's Disease and Dementia: What Everyone Needs to Know* provides an accessible question-and-answer format primer on this disease that touches so many lives.

HIGHLIGHTS

1. Approximately 28 million baby boomers are expected to develop some sort of dementia. More than 5.5 million Americans are living with Alzheimer's. That's about 70 percent of people with dementia. The number is expected to triple within the next few decades.

2. While people are most familiar with Alzheimer's disease, more than 100 types of dementia are documented.

3. The Alzheimer's Disease Bill of Rights developed by Virginia Bell and David Troxel helps dementia sufferers develop a sense of independence, exercise their right to be informed of their condition, and leverage opportunities for engagement.

4. Dementia doesn't signal the end of learning, but rather requires new types of learning.

5. Different types of learning, some of which promote neuroplasticity, include procedural learning, physical learning, experiential learning, novelty learning, and emotional learning.

6. Professional caregivers with experience in interacting with dementia patients will become even more important in senior living settings.

CHAPTER 12

THE ROLE OF SUSTAINABILITY IN SENIOR LIVING

Sustainability, ensuring the future of life on Earth, is an infinite game, the endless expression of generosity on behalf of all.
~Paul Hawken

When it comes to *The Art of Living*, the emphasis on eating well and living well by residents can't eclipse the needs of others to do just the same. That's where sustainability comes in.

Many residents of today's senior living communities may remember the days of rationing during World War II, when there just weren't enough resources to go around. People stood in line for sugar, flour, and other necessities. Even now, as the drain on future resources threatens to be just as intense, some question if we aren't headed for rationing again. One way we can obviously escape a future of ever-dwindling resources is to take steps now to reduce, reuse, and recycle.

At Tuscan Gardens, we are committed to conserving the earth's resources so that our food, water, and energy needs for today are met without compromising the ability of future generations to meet their own needs tomorrow.

All organizations, even senior living communities, need to give careful consideration to sustainability and environmental responsibility. As ecological concerns increase in severity, look for the government to increase regulations and legislation. By taking steps now, your community will be seen as residing on the forefront, making sustainable choices, and doing the right thing long before it was mandated or required.

Tuscan Gardens takes steps to implement programs that are not only good for residents, but also good for the environment, including ones for recycling and waste reduction. Our commitment to providing a sustainable workplace and environment promotes health and well-being here on our campus and within our communities. We seek to identify partners who have a similar commitment to sustainability, as well as educate current partners who have yet to take that step, helping them grow toward a sustainable portfolio of products and programs.

Some ways sustainability can be implemented include:

- Managing kitchen processes in such a way as to reduce the amount of energy and water used in food storage and preparation.

- Aligning menus with the availability of produce from your local area.

- Increasing purchasing of organic and fair trade products, including coffee and tea from sustainable agriculture, ocean caught and farmed sustainable seafood, locally raised dairy and eggs, and locally grown produce in season. Note: Choosing fresh over frozen products is the more sustainable choice. However, when frozen products must be used, thawing in refrigerator versus running water over the frozen food prevents waste.

- Analyzing and reducing delivery frequency.

- Supporting fair farming and trade practices.

- Identifying, reporting and repairing water leaks.

- Minimizing food waste through recycling, recovering, and/or composting pre- and post-consumer organic and non-organic waste materials.

- Using heat recovery and air conditioning economizers.

- Using low-flow aerators on sinks, ENERGY STAR® appliances, and water-conserving rinse spray heads.

- Using products that are recyclable or made from recycled materials.

- Reducing the use of chemicals or using environmentally friendly "green" chemicals in dishwashing and cleaning.

- Choosing items that minimize packaging or use natural materials and biodegradable packaging.

- Incentivizing residents or team members to use reusable products, like drink mugs.

- Sourcing disposable products that have a lighter environmental impact than their conventional counterparts, such as biodegradable items or those manufactured using less petroleum.

- Promoting the use of reusable items (china, silver, glassware) as the default when possible and using biodegradable or recycled-content service ware and trays where china is not feasible.

- Reduce, reuse and/or recycle all disposables such as plastic, aluminum cans, cardboard, glass, paper or metal, including deployment and collection of recycling carts.

- Using 100% post-consumer recycled content paper items and one-at-a-time napkin dispensers.

- Converting appropriate kitchen waste, such as leftover oil or grease into bio-diesel fuel for farm machinery.

- Reducing paper usage with linen napkins.

- Leveraging economical office practices such as using recycled paper and printing or copying on both sides, turning off monitors when not in use and gray scale printing when possible.

Tuscan Gardens is exploring some fascinating sustainability initiatives at its different locations. We are vetting the concept of putting solar panels on the roof of our Palm Coast community due to that fact that we have a great deal of roof line that isn't visible from the street or resident areas. In this way, we can continue to embrace the authenticity we strive for from a branding standpoint while still possibly reaping the rewards of a partially solar powered campus.

We also are exploring incorporating hydroponics into our gardening model at every site. With the proper hydroponic setup, one acre under a greenhouse, provides sufficient hydroponic growth to support 150 residents plus associates. In fact, one acre under cover of a climate-controlled greenhouse, produces an equivalent crop to six acres of open land. Depending upon the individual site, we will have some type of hydroponics – we've even explored putting a greenhouse on the roof of one building!

What this all boils down to is that we take the residents desire to know where their food comes from very seriously. While many communities reference actual farms on their menus, ideally, we look forward to the day we can say that everything comes from our property.

FOOD

We've already talked at length about sustainability as it pertains to growing fresh fruits and vegetables on site in "Chapter 8: Bringing the Outside In."

When and where this is impossible, local sourcing is the next best option. Buying from small, sustainable, and non-commercial farms allows for better quality ingredients. Supporting local farmers not only supports small businesses, but it eases carbon footprints by reducing the fossil fuels and transportation necessary to bring food to the premises.

Increased media attention on food safety makes people increasingly concerned about where their food comes from. Food grown in a region and served to consumers in that same region just makes good sense.

This "farm to table" philosophy emphasizes products that are sustainably grown, processed and procured, considering social and ethical values as well as environmental ones. Smart ways to celebrate this include incorporating more prep and refrigeration space and installing produce washing sinks and systems for cleaning farm direct produce off the loading dock.

In addition to choosing fresh, seasonal, and locally grown foods, sourcing items in ethical and responsible ways that support community development and help move the food onto a sustainable path is imperative. This includes purchasing foods that are:

- **Cage-free**. Cage-free is a certification standard for eggs that encourages greater space for commercially laying hens. Scientists have found that mortality and disease rates are higher in non-cage-free facilities and their environmental footprint is higher. However, cage-free certification does carry an added cost.

- **Humanely raised**. This includes free range (no gestation crates) meats from animals raised in ways that protect their health and wellbeing and minimize the use of antibiotics and other chemicals.

- **Sustainably caught.** Sustainably caught fish and seafood is obtained from properly managed wild fisheries and aquaculture facilities operated to protect natural fish populations and the surrounding environment. Ideally seafood should be certified by either the Marine Stewardship Council or the Global Aquaculture Alliance's Best Aquaculture Practices Program.

- **Fairly traded**. Fair trade/responsible trade products contribute to an improved quality of life in agricultural regions. Two certification systems used to identify these products sourced from tropical regions includes Fair-Trade Certified and Rainforest Alliance Certified.

- **Organically grown**. Organically grown means the grower used no synthetic pesticides and fertilizers.

- **Sustainably grown.** Sustainable growing techniques use agricultural practices that protect natural habitat, conserve energy, restore soil health, and protect water quality.

Purchasing foods that are raised, caught or grown in ethical ways encourages a more robust market for these types of items, which directly affects the people and environments where these goods are produced. It also helps end users feel confident in, and connected to, the production of the food and beverages they consume.

You can get your residents onboard by conducting a series of cooking demonstrations that demonstrate the benefits of local, sustainably grown, and healthy food options. Consider printing materials that promote your sustainability initiatives or share information about menu items prepared from locally sourced produce. Make sure you effectively communicate your sustainability goals to residents and the team. Offer incentives around sustainability achievements.

SUSTAINABLE PRODUCTS

The use of reusable products, as well as low-environmental-impact disposable products can make a big difference in any senior living community's sustainability efforts. Some examples include:

- **China, silver, and glass vs. disposable serving ware**. Using reusable items rather than disposable polystyrene or Styrofoam items is a sustainable choice. While washing does use natural resources, it doesn't outweigh the benefits of choosing items that can be used multiple times and are manufactured of non-toxic materials.

- **Reusable mugs.** Reusable mugs encourage patronage of your onsite coffee spot. Incentivize their use with promotions, such as low-cost refills.

- **Sustainable materials**. Sustainable materials such as paper, molded fiber, bagasse and Polylactic Acid (PLA) are good choices for food containers and serving ware.

  - *Paper items that are wholly compostable and biodegradable are preferred, particularly when manufactured from 100% recycled content.*

+ *Compostable can liners.*

+ *Biodegradable molded fiber pieces, for protective packaging, food service trays, and beverage carriers, are made from 100% recycled corrugated fiberboard and newspaper.*

+ *Bagasse is the fiber that remains after the extraction of juice from sugarcane or sorghum. Additional fibers from reed, bamboo, and hemp are also used in bagasse production.*

+ *PLA products generally are made from the starch in a genetically modified field corn that is not intended for human consumption. By using the biopolymer form of PLA, post-consumer composting can be achieved. PLA items can be used in place of Styrofoam and other plastics.*

RECYCLING

Whenever an item is introduced into your solid waste stream, in other words "disposed of," the far-reaching consequences include wasting the energy, labor, and materials used to produce the item; taking space in the landfill which impacts human health and the environment; and contributing to greenhouse gas emissions.

Reducing product usage or recycling products provides several positive results such as preventing greenhouse gas emissions, decreasing pollutants and saving energy. By reducing the need for new disposal facilities, the cost of waste to the environment and business is lowered and processes are streamlined and efficiency increased.

No single waste management approach is suitable for managing all waste streams in all circumstances. That's why the Environmental Protection Association (EPA) developed a hierarchy ranking the most environmentally sound strategies for municipal solid waste. The hierarchy demonstrates the key components of the EPA's Sustainable Materials Management (SMM).

SMM is a systemic approach to using and reusing materials more productively over their entire lifecycles. It represents a change in how our society thinks about the use of natural resources and environmental protection. By examining how materials are used throughout their lifecycle, an SMM approach seeks to:

- Use materials in the most productive way with an emphasis on using less.

- Reduce toxic chemicals and environmental impacts throughout the material lifecycle.

- Assure we have sufficient resources to meet today's needs and those of the future.

How our society uses materials is fundamental to our economic and environmental future. Global competition for finite resources will intensify as world population and economies grow. More productive and less impactful use of materials helps our society remain economically competitive, contributes to our prosperity and protects the environment in a resource-constrained future.

SOURCE REDUCTION

Source reduction, also called waste prevention, reduces waste at the source. Some ways source reduction is demonstrated is through reusing or donating items, buying in bulk, reducing packaging, redesigning products, and reducing toxicity. In terms of manufacturing, source reduction may include light weighting packaging, reuse, and remanufacturing. The positive by products of source reduction includes saving natural resources, conserving energy, reducing pollution, and reducing waste toxicity.

In terms of food waste, source reduction can be achieved by proper purchasing, preparing, and portioning of food. While zero food waste might be difficult to achieve, reducing food waste to a minimum and composting what little remains is a great idea. Composting food waste, which includes uneaten portions of meals and excess from food preparation activities, benefits the environment and reduces items in your solid waste stream. From a weight perspective, food waste is the heaviest waste generated and occupies over 30% of landfill space.

Benefits of composting include reducing landfill volume and odor and reducing track traffic, fossil fuel use and emissions from hauling.

FOOD RECOVERY CHALLENGE

Participating in the EPA's Food Recovery Challenge (FRC) helps reduce pre-consumer waste, lowers costs associated with compost hauling and processing, and partners you with local community outreach organizations to donate excess foods and leftovers to prevent waste and serve those in need.

As an FRC participate, your community pledges to improve its sustainable food management practices and report results. The FRC is part of EPA's SMM. Using the Food Recovery Hierarchy, as depicted in Image 3, helps you to prioritize your actions to prevent and divert wasted food.

Image 3

Any business or organization can join the FRC as a participant or endorser. Benefits include:

• Reducing your environmental footprint.

• Helping your community by donating nutritious, leftover food to feed hungry people, not landfills.

• Saving money by purchasing less and lowering waste disposal fees.

• Gaining visibility by having your name listed on the EPA's website.

• Receiving recognition through awards and social media.

• Obtaining free technical assistance in the form of webinars, an online database, and resources to help you plan, implement and track your activities, as well as a free climate change report to highlight your positive effect on the environment.

SOLID WASTE STREAMS

The solid waste stream within any senior living community holds the potential for improving the environment and uncovering opportunities for capturing hidden revenue. Few facilities succeed in maximizing the income simply because they are more than willing to pay for disposal of items, which, when properly disposed of, can be recycled and result in rebates.

Establishing a strong recycling program, including properly sized containers conveniently located at point of generation for solid waste, can allow you to capture more than 70% of disposed items. Using clear can liners for your solid waste receptacles allows you to monitor the items being placed in the waste stream and ensure compliance.

Increased fuel costs, landfills at capacity and higher costs at waste-to-energy facilities have all done their part to push solid waste disposal fees higher. In the recent past, per ton disposal rates have doubled in some of the highest occupancy areas of the country. Considering those higher disposal rates and the equally high recycling rebates, creating a program that segregates and recycles appropriate items minimizes your volume and extends the life of landfills.

Structure any solid waste disposal contract in the most advantageous way for your operations. Pay only for what you discard and specify a pick-up schedule based on your timing, not the disposal companies'. Many facilities are required to adhere to a set schedule, whether their receptacles are full or not. Also, don't pay a flat "per pull" rate, rather pay a per-ton fee based on actual weight. Considering transportation costs, pulling only when full benefits you and the disposal company.

Knowing what's recyclable is the first step in creating a recycling program. Generally items that are free from contamination and can be collected in quantity and economically transported to a processor or end user have the best recycling potential.

The following materials tend to be the most common recyclables:

- Paper including shredded documents

- Corrugated containers (cardboard): provided contaminants are removed, boxes are flattened, and pieces are tied or baled together

- Glass such as beverage containers separated by color

- Electronic waste and batteries

- Metal/scrap waste, including aluminum and tin/steel cans, aluminum foil, and other scrap metals

- Plastic separated by resin type

- Vegetation and green waste from landscaping activities

Here are a few things to consider about the different items from within your solid waste stream.

Municipal statutes typically mandate the recycling of cans and bottles. The city or county government in which your community is located will typically provide a pick-up schedule for these items. Place collection receptacles in "point of generation" locations such as kitchens and dining areas. Place one in the area where items from bused tables are collected and one in the food prep area where cans are opened.

You might also like to locate bins near any vending areas or break rooms. The key is to make recycling simple. If the receptacles are conveniently placed, people will use them.

Recycle paper in areas where enough volume is generated and space allows for recycling containers. Using traditional blue bins with no can liners helps people differentiate between garbage cans and recycling receptacles. Areas that generate the largest volumes of paper such as business offices warrant a recycled paper bin. Removing paper from your waste stream reduces volume and generally provides recycled paper rebates. You may be permitted to mix paper with recycled cardboard (discussed below). Be sure to ask your waste stream vendor about it. Large mixed paper/cardboard carts may be able to be located near the point of generation to prevent double handling.

Confidential document waste tends to be overly high due to staff not realizing what constitutes confidential documentation. As the second highest costing waste stream (after regulated medical waste), it's important to properly classify this item. Disposing of confidential documents cost four times as much as generic solid waste. Because team members don't understand the high costs, they may dump any office paper as "confidential" when it more likely is simply recycled paper. This most frequently happens when purging files or cleaning out filing cabinets. Clearly identify what is and what isn't confidential will help control both volume and cost.

Carefully consider the confidential document contractor's practices. They are not required to shred onsite, only to provide you with documentation that the materials were properly disposed of and their security maintained until the point of destruction. A per-container rate is typically easier to monitor and more effective than paying for the time contractors' staff spend onsite.

The vast majority of inventory items delivered to your community arrive in some sort of corrugated (cardboard) containers, including food, paper goods, and cleaning supplies. Proper cardboard disposal can result in rebates based on weight. Many solid waste companies want you to remain in the dark about current market value of cardboard. They position their removal of your cardboard free of charge as a favor to you. In this way, they receive the full rebate being paid by the mill by whoever purchases the cardboard from them.

You can find published cardboard rebates, which are updated monthly. This will allow you to track the amount you should be receiving based on market conditions. Furthermore, removing cardboard from your solid waste stream reduces your volume and weight, which results in additional savings.

Metal recycling tends to be a one-off proposition, but recycling it when you do have the volume can return significant savings. Any infrastructure upgrades such as replacing ventilation systems or resident room remodeling may generate bulk metal waste.

Chances are it's not cost effective to maintain a separate open container for metal, be sure to request one whenever you are transitioning a lot of equipment. You will save on the cost of a dumpster each time you have your vendor pull a full metal container. An average 30-yard open-top container can cost up to $700. Mixed metal containers may pay about $85 per ton at scrap metal yards. Other metals such as copper or stainless steel carry an even higher payback.

In most municipalities, batteries are prohibited from being disposed of in the waste stream in order to protect the environment. Battery recycling at your community requires separation by type: Alkaline (from small electronics), Lead Acid (from back-up power supplies for emergency lighting and other applications), and Ni-Cad and Lithium (both are used in maintenance equipment and biomedical devices). Battery collection should be located near your engineering or facility management department. Except for lead acid batteries, all others are small and can be collected in 30-gallon drums.

Lead Acid batteries have a long-life cycle so the disposal volume is less frequent and regular. You may change these out on a periodic basis, generating a larger volume at a single point in time. Lead Acid batteries can be collected on a skid and shrink wrapped for disposal.

Instituting a recycling program at your community doesn't have to be difficult. Select a person to head up the program preferably an enthusiastic and ecologically-minded individual. This team member with be the point person that other employees, residents, vendors, and contractors work with. Ask this person to form a small recycling team with ideally with representatives from your administrative/executive, procurement, housekeeping, food, and facility management departments. This team will plan, implement, and manage the program.

Have the team conduct a waste assessment to determine the types of recyclable items that your community generates. You can't make an accurate collection plan without understanding what you should collect. Use the baseline data from the waste assessment to measure your progress in waste reduction and meeting your recycling goals.

Speaking of waste reduction goals, obtain a copy of the EPA's Business Guide for Reducing Solid Waste. It's available online from the EPA's website and contains information on setting your waste reduction goals.

Once in place, train your team and residents on your community's recycling program. Training is essential for changing overall behavior that will contribute to your program's success as well as have an exponential impact within your community.

WATER AND HOUSEKEEPING

Of all the water present on earth, 97.5% is unfit to drink. Of the 2.5% that is consumable water, one third remains frozen in the glaciers and polar ice. The water left for human use is roughly 1% of the total water on earth.

Considering that up to 9% of a senior living community's budget is directed toward water and utilities, reducing your spend through conservation and reduction efforts just makes good business sense.

One place where the greatest amount of water seems to be expended is in the area of housekeeping. Using excess water in housekeeping activities not only wastes water, it often increases the risk of employee injury and/or resident injury through slip and falls.

The sustainable choice for cleaning is microfiber, both mops and cleaning cloths. They provide a superior clean over traditional wet-loop mops, as well as saving time, labor, water, and chemicals. In addition to saving water and chemicals, staff members suffer reduced physical strain. A full bucket of traditional cleaning solution for a wet-loop mop can weigh more than 20 pounds and must be changed up to seven times per day. Microfiber requires only two gallons of cleaning solution. Replacing mop heads frequently means less solution is needed and it may only need to be changed once per day. Mopping with microfiber uses .6 gallons of water for every two to three resident rooms mopped versus 2.5 gallons of water with traditional mops, saving 73% of water. Microfiber can last up to 500 launderings when washed properly; traditional mop heads only last through 75 launderings on average.

On the whole, green cleaning focuses on minimizing exposure to harmful chemicals and contaminants, thereby enhancing comfort and health, while minimizing environmental impact.

Green chemicals are developed to reduce total impact on the environment. Beyond the actual chemical formulations and efficacy, the products are evaluated from the standpoint of how they affect natural resources (water and energy), how packaging affects the environment and the safety of the end user.

Looking for Green Seal products is an easy way to ensure environmentally sound cleaning solutions. Green Seal is a nonprofit organization and a pioneer in promoting a sustainable economy. The Green Seal is an easily identifiable mark to represent proven green products and services. Green Seal environmentally friendly cleaning products include non-caustic and non-corrosive general-purpose cleaners, glass cleaners, neutral bathroom cleaners, and zinc-free floor products.

Using highly concentrated green chemicals also helps reduce water usage. Not only do concentrated products use less packaging (taking less landfill space) and reduce shipping costs, but also decrease energy and emissions on shipment, packaging, and disposal. When diluted at optimal level, these products prevent overuse and waste of chemicals.

Please note that if your community seeks LEED certification, you must have a green cleaning policy. The U.S. Green Building Council (USGBC) revised its LEED standard to make green cleaning a prerequisite. To obtain LEED certification, you will need to show that a comprehensive green cleaning program is in place with clear performance goals, including the following:

- **LEED Green Cleaning Criteria #1** – A statement of purpose describing what the policy is trying to achieve from a health and environmental standpoint, focusing on cleaning chemicals and employee training at a minimum.

- **LEED Green Cleaning Criteria #2** – A contractual or procedural requirement for operations staff to comply with the guidelines, including a written program for training and implementation.

- **LEED Green Cleaning Criteria #3** – A clear set of acceptable performance level standards by which to measure progress or achievement such as policies and procedures designed to minimize the use of chemicals, solvents, and water, a program focused on removing building pollutants by implementing preventive measures to contain unwanted contaminants from entering and traveling through the indoor environment and by using green cleaning processes, cleaning products, and equipment to minimize undesirable exposure to indoor occupants.

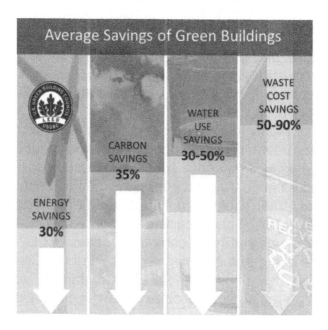

Perhaps the biggest component in defining and executing a workable sustainability program is changing hearts and minds. Your associates and even your residents are a big part of making sustainability a success. Seek culture change. Create initiatives in which everyone works together. Offer rewards, knowing that the biggest reward is to the planet and future generations.

HIGHLIGHTS

1. As ecological concerns increase in severity, look for the government to increase regulations and legislation. Take steps now to be viewed as a community that resides on the

forefront, makes sustainable choices, and does the right thing before it's required.

2. Local sourcing supports farmers and reduces the carbon footprint.

3. Sourcing items in ethical and responsible ways supports community development and helps move the food onto a sustainable path. This includes purchasing foods that are cage-free, humanely raised, sustainably caught, fairly traded, organically grown, and sustainably grown.

4. Recycling programs not only are good for the environment, but may generate revenue.

5. Using reusable products, as well as low-environmental-impact disposable products can make a big difference. Consider using china, silver, and glass versus disposables.

6. Green cleaning minimizes exposure to harmful chemicals and contaminants, enhancing comfort and health.

CHAPTER 13

CREATING COMMUNITY, CONVERSATION & CULTURE

A people without the knowledge of their past history, origin
and culture is like a tree without roots.
~Marcus Garvey

To fully support *The Art of Living*, it's necessary to recruit, hire, and train individuals who have a passion for this type of work and aspire to perform at the very highest level. Highly engaged and personally fulfilled workers deliver exceptional service on an ongoing basis to residents and each other.

One way to get that type of exceptional service is to create a corporate culture to which people fervently desire to belong. While my operational background as a CEO is not related to Senior Living, it is substantial and it emanates from multiple million-dollar businesses in multiple industries. In every such business, it was critical to create a unique culture and inspire workers to embrace it.

A common discussion in any realm of business, from corporate boardrooms to business classrooms, is about the purpose of a company. Two basic views prevail. A corporation exists either to provide a rewarding customer experience or to reward shareholders. Of course, no company is going to shout, "Shareholder Satisfaction Comes First!" in its advertising. But the fact is that, experientially, a thriving business maintains and cultivates happy customers and happy shareholders. In the case of a senior living community, it's vital to provide a rewarding resident experience that simultaneously rewards shareholders, if it is a for-profit enterprise, and stakeholders.

Who are our stakeholders? – the resident, surely, but also the resident's family, particularly the decision makers. These individuals usually hold Power of Attorney and are generally referred to as POA. While all family members are major influencers and involved jointly in decision making for the prospective resident, it's the POAs who have final say. All must be incorporated in the value chain.

The associates also are stakeholders, as are any debt and equity capital providers. It's essential that they also receive a rewarding experience, monetary or otherwise.

Another wider experience should be incorporated into every business operation. We call it the Ultimate Enterprise Experience (UEE). The goal of the UEE is to develop and operate an organization that provides a rewarding experience for itself by delivering a rewarding experience to others —in a labor-efficient and cost-effective way. This is a philosophy of, what I call, *enlightened self-interest.*

It operates on the premise that when you satisfy the objectives of other constituencies, you satisfy and meet your own. It's not a bad philosophy for life, either.

But how can a company, or in our case a senior living community, whose primary concern is its own survival, reconcile this self-serving instinct with such timeworn slogans as "The Resident Comes First!" and "Resident Satisfaction Is Job One"? Aren't these two horses pulling the corporate wagon in opposite directions?

ADDING ASSOCIATES TO
THE EXPERIENCE EQUATION

Traditionally the "others" in the definition has been limited to delivering a rewarding experience to, externally, the residents and, internally, *shareholders.*

However, the rewarding experience must be taken a step further — to include another internal constituency, its employees. At Tuscan Gardens, we refer to these individuals as "associates." Your associates *must* perceive a reward. Their day-to-day employment must be a rewarding experience in order to meet the needs of the residents and reward them. Higher revenues then provide a rewarding experience to the shareholders. The UEE becomes a three-legged stool of reward on which your success rests.

Arguably, along with associates in meeting the needs of residents, yet another constituency must be satisfied as well. Vendors become our partners, supporting us in providing the goods and services we offer. It behooves us, therefore, to make sure they receive a rewarding experience as well.

Jeffery Pfeffer refers to the chain effect of what can go wrong in his book *The Human Equation*. In a downward spiral, all parties are negatively affected when associates are not having a rewarding experience. If associates are not happy, customer service suffers to the point that customers are not having a rewarding experience. As business declines accordingly, shareholders ultimately suffer as the value of their stock declines — certainly not a rewarding experience!

The prerequisite of a UEE, of course, is having or founding a business organization that takes advantage of a business opportunity. The entrepreneur discovers a product or service need in the marketplace that a business operation can meet. Or the owner of an ongoing company can expand or divert resources to satisfy a new market need.

REWARDING EXPERIENCES FOR SHAREHOLDERS

Rewards for shareholders are virtually self-explanatory. Holders of company shares expect to see their investment grow, and may also expect a periodic distribution of dividends as tangible reward for their stock purchases. A robust stock compliments shareholders for their wisdom and foresight in buying the stock. Professor Michael E. Porter of Harvard Business School, perhaps the most widely read management strategist in the world today, insists that the only objective of an enterprise is to enhance and maximize shareholder value.

REWARDING EXPERIENCES FOR ASSOCIATES

Providing a rewarding experience for the organization is a

little more complex. Every enterprise will have a unique definition of that experience. It could simply be profit-driven. Associates of a company enjoying enormous profits can certainly be rewarded with a share of those profits in the form of handsome wages, generous benefits or even ownership.

Speaking of benefits, one senior living community has taken their incentive program to attract and keep employees to a new level. English Meadows Senior Living Communities, based in New River Valley, Virginia, has included in its 2017 employee benefits package an opportunity for long-time employees to live free when the time comes. The benefit promises free senior living to English Meadows employees at the campus where they currently work, based on the total number of years of service. For example, employees with 20 years of service will receive one year of free care, with an additional year at the 30-year and 40-year service level.

Currently, nine employees qualify for some level of free care with approximately 25 more employees becoming eligible over the next few years. In addition to this unique benefit, the revamped package includes free health insurance for employees who have been with the company three years or more, free disability, maternity pay options, and a matching 401(k) for both full-time and part-time workers.

However, rewards for associates extend well beyond a windfall IPO or fat pay envelope. Whole libraries have been written on how to develop more effective management practices, better employer-employee communication, and the importance of valuing the associate and soliciting associate input in management decisions. Rewards in this area could also extend to meeting the personal and familial needs of associates, such as offering daycare facilities, sports, fitness, and recreational programs and employee incentive programs.

Associates can also receive a rewarding experience that emanates from the service their company offers, or pride in its product. Employees of a pharmaceutical company, for example, can take justifiable pride in producing a cancer-fighting drug. Thousands of aerospace workers in Florida, Texas, and elsewhere have taken enormous pride in being part of the space program. The tight-knit community of engineers, technicians, and support people at NASA regard themselves as members of a greater family, to the point that every successful mission is a personal triumph — while each shuttle disaster is a personal, heartbreaking tragedy.

Cirque du Soleil, the internationally acclaimed pantomime circus, designed its entire building so that all workspaces have internal windows looking out into the training and rehearsal areas. Associates, no matter what their function, can look up from mundane administrative tasks and be refreshed and reminded of the spectacular end product their labors help support.

In addition, Cirque du Soleil designed its headquarters building incorporating materials that remind everyone there of the group's origins as street performers. The liberal use of circus props and artifacts reinforces associate awareness of and pride in their organization.

When I ran my prior multi-million dollar company, our seminar division routinely sent individual associates out into the field to attend our three-day training programs. Not only did they benefit from the program knowledge itself, but they sat side-by-side with our customers and studied the material with them. It gave our associates the opportunity to see firsthand the quality of the value proposition, the value that the customers received through the instruction we provided.

For an industry that continually bemoans the dearth of workers and worries about engaging millennials, senior living has a unique associate value proposition that it fails to capitalize upon – that of making a difference. For most millennials it isn't about the money; it's about contributing to something bigger. Millennials seek a greater reason for doing what they are doing.

I found this "contribution factor" to be a very accurate component of a rewarding experience for associates. That's why, when running my prior company, our turnover was the lowest in the region. Categorized as a large business, we had the lowest attrition rate three years running according to an independent survey conducted by our local newspaper. That's what happens when you create an environment where associates know where their win lies, what their contribution is, and how they are rewarded when they do contribute.

At the end of the day, we need to feel good about what we do. We have to put out a good product or service in a responsible way, marketed with balanced and truthful representations, sold effectively, and supported with conviction.

Rewarding experiences for associates are also driven by the degree of value top management puts on its workforce. The corporate culture not only helps define what the company is and what it stands for, but also the type of relationship that exists between the boardroom and the mail room.

Just as each individual associate must consider his or her job a rewarding experience, the company must reward itself — with an enterprise-wide rewarding experience. One large Florida residential-development firm has installed a large bell in its conference room. Every time a house is sold, the bell is tolled. While each individual feels the joy of reward, the corporate entity also savors the sound of the bell as another small victory in a tough housing industry.

Let's look at this example of employee reward. An employee of WD-40 — we'll call him Wade — moved his family from Chicago to San Diego so that he could join the WD-40 team there. Wade loved the team in San Diego and enjoyed his new work environment. His family, meanwhile, tried adapting to life in San Diego, but never made the adjustment. For several reasons, they missed life in Chicago.

Wade acquiesced to his family's feelings and found a job with another company back in the Chicago area, doing what he'd been doing in San Diego. Wade and his family then returned to Chicago. After two years there, he realized that his "corporate heart" was in San Diego at WD-40. Even though his family didn't consider it home, he took an opportunity to return to WD-40 on the West Coast because of the rewarding experience that he had received working there.

There are similar stories throughout the corporate world, a growing body of evidence that companies are able to create that Unique Enterprise Experience —giving the best possible experience to customers and shareholders by keeping their associates rewarded and fulfilled at several levels.

REWARDING EXPERIENCES FOR RESIDENTS

What about the delivery of a rewarding experience to prospective and existing customers or, in our case, residents? A rewarding experience for a resident derives from the concept of a value proposition. Whether in an executive sales presentation, an automobile showroom or the produce section of a supermarket, there must be a value proposition every time a business offer is made. Customers must perceive that they are receiving value — paying a fair price for what they are getting. Price point must be commensurate with perceived quality, but never higher than that quality.

A customer's rewarding experience begins with a company's ability to provide good-quality products or services. If the new cell phone, barbecue grill or cable service doesn't work, the potential for customer reward is in immediate jeopardy. If the resident is promised filet mignon for breakfast, lunch, and dinner, yet receives a hamburger, the rewarding resident experience is in jeopardy.

If the customer feels that the company is doing its best to rectify a bad situation that customer may be on the way to feeling true customer satisfaction. If that perception lasts, customer satisfaction matures into customer loyalty — a truly rewarding experience for both the customer and the company.

In the marketplace, if customer demands, the economy and technology all stood still, customer satisfaction would be a snap. All management would have to do would be to find the optimum combination of customer "hot buttons" and keep pushing them *ad infinitum*. In the real world, the dynamics of all these variables require corporations to constantly adapt. They must shift their strategies continuously to meet new demands, conditions, and contingencies while clinging to their core values and competencies.

THE CORPORATE MODEL

Companies, consciously or unconsciously, begin operations with a business model. Sometimes it is only expressed by a founder who says, "I want to start a company that..." That model might be providing quality products at low cost to a mass market, or offering customized services to narrow niche markets. The business model, the types of products or services a company offers and to whom, defines the company and what it does. The model of a corporation is perhaps the easiest element to define. It's the answer to the question, "What do you do?" The questions that follow are more abstract and elusive and more critical to long-term survival.

When creating Tuscan Gardens, my business model was to offer a senior living community with luxurious environments and personal care equivalent to a concierge service. The idea was to offer incredibly spacious and comfortable private living spaces and services designed to provide the highest quality of life in an atmosphere of joyfulness, caring, and intimacy. Nestled in residential communities and far removed from institutional care facilities, Tuscan Gardens offers all the amenities residents could ever want, equal to or even more luxurious than those enjoyed throughout their entire lives.

If the business model delineates what a company is, its culture defines *who* it is. The culture is the soul and spirit of the company, an intangible that generates employee pride and enthusiasm for the job beyond the quality of the product or service.

THE CORPORATE MISSION

Aside from staying profitable, great companies have a larger purpose to their operations, the expression and application of some core values. This purpose is expressed in a term that, unfortunately, has been trivialized through misuse: The Mission Statement.

In a thriving company, it's vital that everyone in the organization stand for something more far-reaching than day-to-day operations, and be guided by more than standards of convenience and situational ethics. That's why so many corporations regale visitors to their lobby with a prominent plaque that proclaims "Our Mission."

Effective, organic mission statements move past the lobby, and are infused into every decision. Such a mission permeates every individual in the organization as well as the corporate culture itself. A working mission dictates the direction a corporation takes, and will ultimately catapult that company toward profitable opportunities.

Many organizations go through the process of developing a mission statement and a set of core values or beliefs. Arguably, a lot of organizations use their mission statements as window dressing, not fully subscribing to the ideals expressed. By contrast, successful companies integrate their mission statements into the decision-making process. They have permeated the corporate culture and each individual involved with the organization.

The message here is that in addition to knowing how a business functions on a basic level, its leaders need to know what their company stands for. A clear understanding of what values and beliefs drive decision-making within the corporation enhances its ability to find and pursue opportunities that it can fully exploit. Then the leaders must make sure that they build that into the fabric of the organization and communicate it relentlessly to all associates, vendors, shareholders, and customers.

THE CORPORATE VISION

Finally, there has to be a vision for what the organization will look like years from now. Providing vision is at once the most fundamental duty of leadership — and often its most difficult, even for top executives.

As a leader, you must create a vision — a clear, simple, reality-based, customer focused/resident focused vision — and communicate it effectively to everyone. Translate your vision into bulleted points. Have your managers write them down and buy into them. A leader's responsibility must be to remove every blinder, every barrier to ensure that vision is first clear, and then adopted as real by everyone in the organization. The greatest victory of a visionary is to capture minds and have them work not just willingly but *enthusiastically* toward achieving your vision.

Vision is brave, strategic thinking. Stretch your horizons. Let your mind soar. Challenge your imagination to make your vision *big*! Otherwise, a small vision is just an idle wish framed in the lobby beside the mission statement.

What do you get when you remove all the physical trappings of a business? You're left with processes, people, and values — otherwise known as corporate culture. It's not the mission statement, it's not the product of an executive team's retreat and it's not the awards hanging on the wall — it is the people and culture.

Culture is a set of values, beliefs, norms or expectations that a company practices on a daily basis. It's the first step toward understanding who you are, realizing what you have, and knowing where you want to be.

A lot of being a part of a culture is unconscious. If you want some interesting perspectives on what your corporate culture is, ask around. Ask prospective associates, a couple of residents, your consultants, and your vendors. Did they "feel" the culture the last time they talked with an associate or visited your premises?

For example, the last time a resident called with an issue, how did they feel about the resolution? Delighted with the experience, or grumbling about bureaucracy? Unfortunately, they might be able to tell you more about your culture than you can. The point is to have a clear understanding of who you are as a company, and harnessing that culture for the purpose of morphing — deliberately evolving in order for your company to thrive, whatever its environment.

You see, culture drives your organization and what it does. It moves employees toward what to think, what to do and how to feel. It's not a "Big Brother" dictatorship, but the fact is that people are influenced by the values, beliefs, and expectations of their environment. Culture evolves constantly too. Today's inspiration can be tomorrow's stumbling block.

In addition, elements of a basically healthy culture can be detrimental to achieving a company's goals and objectives. Avoiding conflict is a good example. Some companies discourage direct confrontation on issues, believing that a façade of harmony is better for those involved than dealing with and exorcising the problem. Like an untreated wound, however, an unresolved issue, whether a policy or operational or personal problem, can fester into a larger crisis. By contrast, once that unhealthy trait is identified and understood, strategies can be initiated that promote truth, honesty, constructive criticism, mediation, healthy discussion, and resolution.

The most visible expressions of culture are artifacts — the design of the building, the company logo, the decor, even what associates wear to work. It's the rituals, slogans, symbols, and celebrations. It's even the company jargon, and the myths and legends of past victories in marketplace wars. What's interesting is how useful these cultural artifacts are in motivating employees toward greater innovation, corporate goals, and objectives.

A COMMUNITY ENGAGED IN ONGOING CONVERSATION

When you meet that one special someone in your life, one of

the most important elements in the relationship is communication. There must be ongoing conversation. If that conversation is absent, the relationship will go nowhere. Your community should be in a constant state of dialogue and communication.

Key to becoming more integrated is conversation among associates. Once an example, a standard, is set that shows the value of conversation, associates will realize the importance of communication, and the overall demeanor of the staff improves.

There must be a climate in the company that encourages truth. It's vital that everyone involved have all the correct information they need to make prudent decisions. At work, as in marriage, the lack of truth, or partial truth, or even withholding facts, is always counterproductive to company relationships.

Information is power, and if that power is held by a few, you will not get the power of the many. The path to truth is found by asking questions rather than giving answers. By asking questions, you're engaging in conversation. Astute questions enable you to dissect a problem or situation without laying blame. From this you will be able to extract information, address the need, and fix the problem.

Communication, of course, works best when the team is in lockstep and looking together toward a bright future. This begins with hiring.

HIRING YOUR TEAM

The numbers are staggering. In little more than 30 years, 88 million seniors will be living in the United States. That's nearly double the number today. Hiring individuals to work with and care for this graying population is now and will be in the future a critical endeavor. Senior living communities seek real solutions for not only attracting and hiring, but also retaining worthy staff members.

According to national senior living research firm Holleran, the so-called "honeymoon" period of high engagement lasts just one year for senior living employees. First-year senior living employees are about 10% more engaged than veterans with a year or more under their belts. However, employees who have worked at a community for two years show similar engagement levels with colleagues of 10 or more years standing. Holleran further reports that reducing turnover during this critical period requires supervisors who demonstrate a high level of engagement, regular feedback on job performance, and outlining a clear roadmap of career progression to show the employee where they might logically end up.

When I entered this industry, I was told in no uncertain terms to expect a 30% to 50% turnover rate, which is industry standard. In fact, according to national senior living provider association, LeadingAge, the average employee turnover for life plan communities rests at 42%. Rather than expecting the worst, I decided to start with a 0% turnover in mind and figure out what I could do to provide a meaningful environment where associates wouldn't want to be anywhere else.

For me, I always think in terms of *hiring talent* rather than just filling positions. When you hire talent, there is a clear understanding of what is expected — defining the "win" for each person in terms of performance measurement. Aside from the glowing resume, what is your gut, your intuition, telling you about how the prospective employee will fit into the organization? Remember — the talent you hire is a competent human being with potential for making the company more successful; the position you fill is just a square on the organizational chart.

I've formulated a specific approach to hiring the best talent. It can be summed up in one simple phrase: You get what you incentivize.

If you pay a higher than ordinary compensation and you incentivize based upon individual as well as community performance, you get not only a higher quality individual, but also both a higher level of individual and team performance in providing deliverables.

If a particular position pays at $8 an hour, pay $9 an hour. If that position generally comes in for $12 an hour, set the rate at $13 an hour. Then, establish a general employment policy which creates individual, departmental, and community-based incentive programs.

This policy has always served me well in that it set the stage for attracting and maintaining the highest quality employee, the highest level of loyalty, the lowest turn-over, and the best reputation in whatever industry that happened to be.

My viewpoint notwithstanding, labor shortages in the senior living industry may do their own part to persuade you to bump up your pay scales.

A report by Hospital and Healthcare Compensation Service shows wages increased for every position in assisted living in 2016. The basis for this report, Hospital and Healthcare Compensation Service's 19th annual survey, included data from 1,300 assisted living communities (1,188 for profit and 124 not for profit).

The largest jump in hourly salaries, 3.75%, came for resident assistants, moving from $10.53 to $10.92. For salaried individuals, marketing representatives enjoyed a 3.67% jump from $44,301 to $45,925.

Top 10 Salaries in 2016

1. CEO/President: $142,704

2. Chief Financial Officer: $97,920

3. Assisted Living Administrator: $77,456

4. Director of Information Technology: $77,321

5. Director of Human Resources: $73,461

6. Director of Nurses: $68,098

7. Resident Care Coordinator: $62,032

8. Director of Marketing: $60,964

9. Memory Care Program Director: $60,276

10. Director of Dining/Food Services: $57,324

   * Source: Hospital and Healthcare Compensation Service

One other comment with regard to paying higher than ordinary compensation: Today's senior has a higher expectation of the quality of care they will receive in a senior living facility. Addressing these expectations requires employing technology with greater frequency and in more sophisticated ways. These technological advances necessitate recruiting staff members with a higher level of education, a greater familiarity with technology, and a willingness to maintain and enhance their facility with technology through ongoing training and development. This higher caliber worker would require a greater pay scale anyway. Facilities also may need to conduct a more extensive evaluation process in recruiting individuals and ascertaining that they have the necessary skills and credentials to leverage technology in the ways needed to enhance the resident experience.

The organization I built at my previous company began with zero sales and zero associates. It grew to $258 million per year in sales with $40 million of free cash flow and 600 associates. We reached the Inc. 100 and 500 three years in a row and were named a top employer locally for three years as well. Our turnover rate was less than 2%. It was so negligible it was not worth counting. This success stemmed from our managerial philosophy and this is what we are operationalizing at Tuscan Gardens.

With Tuscan Gardens, we have built an incredibly effective website with a robust career section. As such, we've had to do very little external recruiting, relying almost entirely on applications received from the website. Once someone visits the career section, they can very clearly see three things:

- **The available positions**

- **The Tuscan Gardens Philosophy**

- **The type of individual we seek to be a part of our family (requirements)**

For those who fall into those dimensions, and instantly feel the tug of "I want to work here!", we issue an across the board invitation to apply.

In all of my businesses, when seeking associates to join the organization, we have established high standards and have adhered to them. Often, I've been chastised by Human Resources professionals who've basically warned me that the standards will make the positions impossible to fill.

For example, in my past forays into food service businesses,

I've required servers to hold high school diplomas, the only exception being for young people who are still in school working to obtain their diplomas. Several people in the staffing industry told me to forget it. They were wrong.

Another example where I didn't lower standards was in requiring associates to be non-smokers. To me, smoking is a waste of time. Smokers want multiple breaks to indulge the habit. The image of associates hanging around the back of a building and tossing butts on the ground is, in a word, classless. That is not consistent with or conducive to the image I want portrayed in any of my businesses.

Tuscan Gardens is a non-smoking campus. I've been told that I'd never fill positions with the requirement that applicants be non-smokers or quit smoking before joining the team. We ask every single interviewee if he or she smokes and, if so, are they willing to quit. Even residents are asked to smoke outside, not within the building.

It doesn't work when the applicant says they are a smoker, but won't smoke at the job. We hire only nonsmokers. You are a nonsmoker today or a nonsmoker the minute you set foot on campus for your first day. My experience is that smokers smoke. They can't go a whole day without indulging. So, I don't want to go through the whole hiring process with an individual who then lights up on their first break on their first day.

Alignment can't be created without making sure the expectations are very clear. The first aspect is being very clear in the ad about the type of people we seek and then very clear in the interview what the job and the culture are all about. In this case, not smoking.

Here's a better alternative across the board with respect to everything: Don't dumb down the standards. Elevate the standards so the people you get are the ones who want to be surrounded by like-minded individuals. That's why a Burger King employee looks significantly different than a Chick-fil-A employee. The latter has established and adhered to standards in the type of person they hire.

One final, yet very compelling reason to hire the absolute best talent you can is that you are laying the foundation for succession planning, an issue which vexes senior living more than other industries. Yes, you work with an aging resident population, but your professional staff is aging right along with them. Few things can be more devastating to a community than when the institutional knowledge retires and disappears.

So many senior living communities are so focused on filling current gaps that they give short shrift to building and developing the leaders of tomorrow. By hiring exceptional talent now and providing cutting edge professional development programs in the future, you take steps to prevent that sort of crisis.

A multi-layered interview process is the next step from phone interviews to in-person screening at the community. In addition to the typical vetting, we require that any potential hire is interviewed personally by Janet or me once they have been approved at the community level. That goes for everyone. We meet everyone from the potential director of finance to the housekeeper.

As mentioned, at Tuscan Gardens, our employees are called Associates. Associates represent the members of the community who are involved in caregiving regardless of what their primary function is. To our way of thinking accountants contribute to caregiving in the same way restaurant servers do, albeit less directly.

It is relatively common in senior living not to have anything other than an offer letter that identifies compensation. Not so at Tuscan Gardens. At the beginning of every associate relationship, we prepare an in-depth Performance Agreement and Employment Agreement that work with and are aligned to the offer letter.

We need to make sure that none of these documents are just pieces of paper. What we seek is vertical alignment from onboarding to performing to ongoing training that descends all the way down to interacting with the residents.

Performance agreements are very substantially intended to produce alignment between who we are advertising for on the site, the ones we are interviewing, the ones we are hiring, and those who are acting inside the community. It lists expectations in terms of culture, organization, personal, and job specific.

This document defines Tuscan Gardens by its principles, protocols, and performance standards. It begins with the Vision and the Mission of the Organization. It gives an Overview of the Community as a goal-driven organization, and defines how an associate can expect to be regarded by the company in terms of trust, dignity, respect, recognition, and support.

Other areas of the Performance Agreement include:

- *Cultural Standards* – These include standards of demeanor and behavior, quality of work, commitments to teamwork and leadership, meeting of deadlines, and general professionalism.

- *Organizational Procedures* – This area covers the accepted steps used to accomplish routine tasks, or rules about communication, tidiness, noise levels, lunch breaks, and other housekeeping practices.

- *Job Title, Description, Job Functions* – These are the specific duties and responsibilities of the individual who signs the Performance Agreement.

- *Empowerments* – This section enumerates areas of authority, accessibility, and responsibility commensurate with the position.

- *Cultural Expectancies* – These are expectations of performance dealing with initiative, leadership, creativity, judgment, resourcefulness, and other subjective skills and talents.

- *Cultural Deliverables* – The associate is charged with performing his or her job with such intangibles as adaptability, self-management, team awareness, effective communication, focus, and other culture-based qualities.

- *Performance Expectancies* – Specific position-related responsibilities. The executive assistant, for example, "will handle routine processes and deliverables in the normal course of the day, without reminders, supervision or management."

- *Performance Deliverables* – This section lists specific tasks to be performed in the normal course of the day, as well as behavioral guidelines appropriate to the associate's position. In the case of the executive assistant, many of these tasks relate directly to assisting the chairman and helping coordinate his events and activities.

213

The Performance Agreement is so associate-specific that it eliminates any doubt or confusion regarding associate performance, attitude, and relationships with other associates or with the company. As has been mentioned, it also provides the metrics for measuring performance, which is addressed and reviewed on an annual basis for all employees, and every six months for executives, including directors and managers.

The performance agreement is the foundation for both the 90-day review and any subsequent annual reviews. Due to its much broader context, associates are measured in relation to the Performance Agreement rather than the more nebulous "how you did as a caregiver." Because it defines expectations as well as cultural alignment, it's a self-immersive method that ensures ongoing alignment with the stated resident experience.

This agreement is the initial step in achieving alignment — from the chairman to the receptionist. As we've indicated, communication is absolutely vital to the health of an enterprise, particularly its alignment. More than 20 years ago, Tom Peters wrote in his breakthrough business work, *In Search of Excellence*, "A remarkably tight — culturally driven/controlled — set of properties marks the excellent companies. Most have rigidly shared values. The action focus...emphasizes extremely regular communication and very quick feedback; nothing gets very far out of line."

Once that performance agreement has been signed, substantial training takes place with regard to what Tuscan Gardens means and what an associate's alignment is within it. This is in addition to job-based training. Initial training certainly embraces a demeanor component.

It can be difficult to teach "class." If you've never been exposed to it, you don't know what it looks like or how to emulate it. What does demeanor look like in a Tuscan Gardens associate? The language you will hear from one of our associates will include phrases like, "How can I assist you?", "My pleasure," and "Absolutely." This demeanor is exhibited from the General Manager right down to the housekeepers. Tuscan Gardens' demeanor is always modeled, always rewarded and always spotlighted.

Modeling, rewarding and spotlighting are topics worthy of spending just a bit more time discussing because of the power they hold to transform not only associates, but residents.

At my prior company, we always held an annual meeting

and at this meeting we presented various awards to individuals for behaviors we wanted reinforced and repeated whether these were sales-related or service-related. The demeanor reward was among the most meaningful, not only in that it rightfully honored a person who admirably exhibited our values, but also that it also highlighted the physical representation of what I desired all associates to achieve. When I would recognize a person as that year's honoree and explain their achievements, I was also telling everyone else in the ballroom, "That's what I want you to do! Model this person!"

Recognizing the behavior you want replicated can also take place within your resident population. At Tuscan Gardens we have a monthly happy hour cocktail party held in the grand room. The purpose is to honor the resident who was the strongest source of referrals. The event begins with appetizers and wine, but culminates in a speech recognizing that key person.

It's particularly important to honor the person and not just the referral(s). I usually make a speech wherein I describe the person without naming him or her. This builds excitement and anticipation. I might say, "This person came to us from the New England area, having decided never to lift another shovel full of snow again. You would probably recognize him by the Boston Red Sox ball cap, his infectious laugh or the work he puts in on the tomato plants in the greenhouse. I'm delighted to honor Joe Jones for being a star referral partner this month with a check for one thousand dollars."

I always have a check printed and ready to hand to the individual. The honoree is delighted and the rest of the crowd wants to be the next honoree. What I've told them effectively is "I want more people just like this person."

So many senior living communities pay $25 or $50 for a referral. Not only do they not present it publicly, they often don't present it at all, rather letting the small stipend become a credit to their account.

If you know your costs for acquiring a resident from the general public, it only makes sense to reward a referral that brings someone into your community without that expense. You now have a trust transference referral from an existing resident. Recognize that with a meaningful sum of money presented in front of the entire community.

Returning to the topic of associates, a formal onboarding

program clarifies expectations and familiarizes staff with a community's culture. Initial training for any specific position should consist of three to five days of intensive information and result in certification at the end of the training for the particular position in which the individual serves. Annual recertification ensures an ever-growing knowledge base of best practices. Ongoing and formalized training benefits the facility and the residents. Two full community training days annually further creates an atmosphere of camaraderie and fellowship.

After someone has been hired, it's critical that you show them that you value them. Nothing does this better than providing a workspace to call their own. A personal workspace sends the message that you see the relationship as permanent (and if you hired right it should be).

A personal workspace creates a meaningful environment. People who work in meaningful environments don't consider working anywhere else. The associate experience is interwoven with the Resident Experience. Associates who are joyfully engaged and participating ultimately benefit the residents.

Engaged associates are a key part of the value proposition. When the enterprise is built to serve the stakeholders (residents, associates, and capital providers) who are all mutually engaged and participating, you create the ultimate enterprise experience.

Employee engagement or associate engagement to use Tuscan Gardens nomenclature refers to the associate's commitment to our organization. Engaged associates exhibit two specific behaviors: 1) They speak positively about their job, supervisors, co-workers, and residents and 2) They work harder and possess attributes that contribute to your success.

The quality of success enjoyed by most businesses can be measured by the quality of people working for them. When people are given an opportunity to contribute in a meaningful way and experience personal and professional growth for themselves, they stay motivated for the long-term. Equip your team with training and education, proper tools and equipment, flexible operational support, and professional management and supervision to keep them engaged while at the same time achieve quality results.

Associates must feel appreciated, valued, and respected for the unique individuals that they are and reminded that they are making a real difference. You must provide sincere recognition for excellence or acknowledge that another employer will be more than happy to do so.

What you are attempting to create is a longevity of experience. We want an associate to be a part of the community long-term because we hate turnover. If you actually want turnover, here's a tip: Don't give the person a permanent space. Point out an empty chair and tell them to sit there "for now." If the owner of that space shows up, shuffle them somewhere else or tell them to find an available spot on their own. That lack of permanence will keep you in the interviewing business for a long time.

Once onboard and trained, associates serve as a community's best and most compelling calling card.

ASSOCIATE PROGRAMMING AND DOCUMENTATION

Speaking of onboarding and training, nothing ensures the success of these initiatives like written programming and documentation. At Tuscan Gardens, we have the following:

- A 3-day Associate Orientation and Training Program

- A 3-day Associate Orientation Manual

- An Associate Recruitment Program

- An Associate Training Program

- A Performance Management Program

- A Project Management Program

- A Formidable Resident Move-In Protocol

- A Proven Resident and Associate Retention Program

DRESS CODE

In order to prevent an institutional atmosphere, uniforms should be avoided. In other words, nothing in the clothing style that is even close to what is expected, ordinary or conventional in Senior Living. In order to evoke the atmosphere of a Ritz Carlton, Four Seasons or even a high-end Hyatt Regency, the dress must be consistent with what you would expect to see in this type of establishment.

Tuscan Gardens encourages street clothes for all associates. Dress code is a cut above what's become known as "business casual." Women wear skirts, dresses and blouses with low heeled, non-skid shoes. Slacks and crisp polo shirts for men along with dress shoes is the dress code. Tasteful jewelry, including necklaces, earrings, and bracelets for women and rings and watches for both men and women. The wearing of perfumes or colognes is consistent with the general expectation, sensitivities, and allergies of the residents.

In outlining the Tuscan Gardens dress code to management at other communities, I have often received quizzical stares. In one such exchange, I was told in no uncertain terms that "Caregivers need to be comfortable." The person rather patronizingly continued by recommending white nurses shoes and scrubs to me, the senior living neophyte.

I returned the quizzical stare and responded, "Why? This is not a hospital. This is a residence for these individuals. We will have no nurses' shoes and no scrubs – not even for the nurses."

At Tuscan Gardens, nurses dress like the non-clinical staff. Somehow the testy person with whom I had this exchange felt like caregivers had to look like caregivers for them to be effective in their roles. The clinical caregivers here (as opposed to the other roles that also provide care) are part of the community. We like to think of them as members of a resident's extended family who are here to support and serve them.

HIGH PERFORMANCE AND LEADERSHIP

Earlier I mentioned how many of my business philosophies were gleaned over 20 years marketing sales and fulfillment events across the country. Considering the annual revenue, associate count and $40 million in free cash flow, the endeavor would be considered, by anyone's definition, a high-performance work environment. And, performance on that level happens only by design. It begins by setting a vision, culture, and mission for team members to embrace.

From there, strategic plans, consisting of product and project charters, are defined to provide a roadmap. Within those plans, clear strategic goals must be set with and the team imbued with the drive to complete them.

The corporate team, in particular the C-suite, is built with their highest and best use in mind. Extraneous tasks are removed to allow single-minded focus on the achievement of strategic goals. Efficient and effective communication protocols between the team streamline maximize productivity.

When it comes to the management teams in specific Tuscan Gardens communities I like to look for seasoned professionals with an entrepreneurial spirit. This type of person has the autonomy to run their unit as their own business and efficiently manage the facilities. They have the trust of upper management to creatively solve problems and the authority to act nimbly, yet can still rely on strong C-Suite support.

It's particularly important for the management team to be continually woven into the Tuscan Gardens community, as well as the community at large, which creates a positive chemistry for residents, visitors, staff, and administration. In doing so, they are able to work collaboratively throughout the campus to anticipate challenges and seek opportunities for continuous improvement, while building open and honest relationships.

Communication between the leadership team may include a weekly video conference call and a monthly full one day meeting. A quarterly recap day with the broader group also takes place and two semi-annual training days for all employees keep everyone in constant alignment.

Operationally, systems are put in place (based on written SOPs) and technological tools leveraged that allow processes to be automated to their greatest extent. Several systems implemented at Tuscan Gardens include a bidding system, purchase order system, CRM, etc.

We've already discussed the employment agreements, performance agreements, and performance evaluations that provide clarity with regard to management expectations and associate progress in meeting and/or exceeding those expectations.

Meetings, rather than being seen as a necessary evil, are organized to be highly effective gatherings that continue to propel the team toward strategic goals. Typical meetings at Tuscan Gardens include weekly PMR meetings, monthly leadership meetings, quarterly board meetings, and semi-annual off-sites.

In closing this section, I'd like to share the processes and protocols mandated at Tuscan Gardens and in all of my business endeavors. They are:

- **Meetings start and end on time – no exceptions**

- **Cell phones and other interruptions are not permitted in meetings**

- **Orderly processes produce orderly results**

- **Listen intently; speak less with minimal interruptions**

- **Not Invented Here (NIH) Syndrome not present here**

- **Deadlines are set in stone**

Some specific meetings which take place at Tuscan Gardens include:

- Community Oversight Team consists of internal executives and key stakeholders within the geographical community in which the specific Tuscan Gardens is located. Meetings occur monthly.

- Each community's management team has a monthly meeting between themselves and Tuscan Gardens' corporate executives.

- For the Project Management Review, the Executive Director, Marketing Director, Activities Coordinator, and Director of Health Services meet weekly with the CEO, Executive Vice President, and or CAO of Tuscan Gardens to review:

  - *KPIs*

  - *Flash Report*

  - *Monthly Financial Reporting: P&L, Budget, and Metrics*

♦ *Crystalize Customer Benefits*

These processes and protocols allow us to deliver a rewarding experience not only to residents, but to associates and capital partners in an efficient and effective manner, and permit us to fulfill our mission to develop and deliver an exceptional resident experience which ensures an elegant, fulfilling, and enriching senior lifestyle immersed in purpose, passion, and joy.

I'd like to close this section with what I call the High-Performance Laws of the Universe. To me these short statements help keep things in perspective and remind me of the type of behaviors I demand of myself and others in delivering a life filled with purpose, passion & joy, for the residents of Tuscan Gardens.

High Performance Laws of the Universe

- **It Is What It Is**

- **This Too Shall Pass**

- **Results Rule, But Intentions Do Matter**

- **Take Personal Responsibility for Everything**

- **Always Do What You Say You're Going To Do**

HIGHLIGHTS

1. Recruit, hire, and train individuals who have a passion for working with seniors and aspire to perform at the very highest level. Highly engaged and personally fulfilled workers deliver exceptional service on an ongoing basis to residents and each other.

2. Aside from staying profitable, great companies have a larger purpose to their operations, the expression and application of some core values. This purpose is expressed in the mission statement.

3. The Ultimate Enterprise Experience is based on providing a rewarding experience to all stakeholders – residents, family members, associates, and shareholders.

4. When it comes to staff, you get what you incentivize.

5. Vertical alignment that begins at onboarding and moves through performing to ongoing training all the way down to interacting with the residents ensures a meaningful culture.

6. The Ultimate Enterprise Experience results from the integrational alignment of community, conversation & culture.

CHAPTER 14

MANAGEMENT SYSTEMS

I have left, for a separate chapter, the all-important subject of how a senior living community is actually managed. In other words, after dealing with all of the architecture, design, culture, technology, food and beverage, landscaping, and so forth, when it comes right down to it, how does the community get managed on a day-to-day basis? Historically, the senior living industry has experienced the following primary business models.

BOARD AND CARE OWNER-OPERATORS

For small owner-operated senior living facilities, typically between six to twenty-four units, the owner tends to be the operator. These are usually called board and care homes, are often sheltered in remodeled single-family and multi-tenant properties, and don't very often have the economics to support operation except by the owner. The advantage of an owner-operator is that the owner has the opportunity to vent his or her effects, creating the sense of place they envision, and executing that vision with intimacy and personal contact with the residents. The disadvantage, of course, is that the resources do tend to be constrained and because of the small size of the facility, limitations on the expertise of the owner tend to make a rich senior experience more problematic. Nonetheless, for countless seniors spread across the entire country, in need of services, execution through owner-operators in a board and care environment is a very viable solution.

THIRD-PARTY OPERATORS

For owners of larger facilities, often as large as 96 to 178

223

units, whether owned by independents, real estate investment trusts (REITs), private equity firms, or non-profit organizations, third-party operators have emerged which don't typically have an ownership interest in the community, but who bring substantial resources and experience to the table.

For independent and non-profit owners, as well as capital providers, such as REITs and private equity firms whose primary objective is to invest capital in hard assets such as in the senior living asset class, management by third-party operators provides an attractive model which reduces the risk of execution for any given community.

In addition to a proven operations platform, third-party operators provide:

- *Wide and deep network:* Large third-party operators have spent years establishing relationships with vendors and suppliers, allowing owners to punch way above their weight.

- *Comprehensive training programs:* Proper and ongoing training is key to retaining associates in this challenging labor market.

- *Professional marketing:* Third party operators have the talent to help owners craft their brand, as well as market that brand in print and online.

- *Scalability:* As an owner grows, either adding communities through mergers or development, a third-party operator has the infrastructure to grow along with them.

- *Experience and best practices:* Success in the senior living industry requires a depth of knowledge that is difficult to get right out of the gate. To be able to rely on a team of experts in several topic areas – sales, marketing, human resources, financial, legal, nutrition, clinical and more – is a tremendous advantage.

- *Quality and consistency:* Very much like your favorite food franchise where you know that the hamburger you eat in Pittsburgh tastes the same as the one you eat in Peoria, third-party operators can provide a consistent experience across one or more communities.

On the other hand, the disadvantage of third-party operators is that they tend to lose in differentiation what they gain in high-level scalability. Very rarely does a senior living community have the economic capacity at the community level to create a corporate infrastructure on the ground. Therefore, when managed through a third-party operator, the third party achieves corporate oversight through a shared services model where the corporate oversite is paid for by sharing "the resource" over multiple communities. With that, however, individual community identity – a.k.a brand or personality – often tends to get compromised, the quality of execution is diminished, and the resident experience becomes commoditized.

For a capital provider looking primarily for financial results, that compromise may very well be acceptable provided that the community delivers the return on investment the financial projections mandate. However, for the independent owner who is committed to the brand promise, as well as the well-being of the seniors, the result of a third-party operator who has no financial stake in the outcome of its delivery and is delivering through a shared services model may not be acceptable.

OWNER-OPERATORS

The third business model which can be found in senior living is in those communities in which the owner is also the operator and can deliver economies of scale. Where that is seen at the largest level is in publicly-traded corporations. The top ten publicly traded corporations in the United States are the following:

Organization	Number of Facilities
Brookdale Senior Living, Inc	1066
Genesis HealthCare	380
HCR ManorCare	280
Holiday Retirement	274
Evangelical Lutheran Good Samaritan Society	268
Golden Living	257
Sunrise Senior Living, Inc.	255

5 Star Quality Care	224
Life Care Centers of America	223
Assisted Living Concepts Inc	202
Consulate Health Care	202

Where you can also find the owner-operator business model is in those senior living companies which have created sufficient economies of scale to operate its own in-house corporate infrastructure. Typically, they tend to be regional, which allows for greater efficiency in operations, optimal understanding of the region, and they tend to own and operate a minimum of five communities.

With respect to the large public companies, they tend to have the advantages that large corporations have: scalability, access to capital and depth of resources. At the same time, they also have the same types of disadvantages that most public corporations have: the need to optimize return on shareholder equity, which sometimes compromises delivery of services to seniors, and institutionalization, which often calcifies performance and personal initiative at the personnel level. At the smaller level, where regional owner-operators own approximately five to fifteen communities, there are distinct advantages. Differentiation of the brand is significant, personal corporate attention minimizes flaws in execution and regional knowledge provides substantial noninstitutionalized flexibility.

On the other hand, despite the advantages of this model, some disadvantages do emerge. As against the public companies and the large third-party operators, for example, the mid-sized regional owner-operators tend to lack the depth and breadth of resources that are so critical to the safeguarding of our seniors, particularly on the health and safety levels. Moreover, to the extent that the economies tend to be more limited, the financial ratios may not necessarily support the level of corporate oversight which would otherwise be preferred or even appropriate.

Nonetheless, management by an owner-operator is not only very viable, but offers the closest to what is a preferred and optimally replicable business model for the management of senior living communities.

COLLABORATIVE MANAGEMENT MODEL

At Tuscan Gardens, our management has been evolving since inception. Since our very first community which consisted of 136 units – 78 assisted living units and 58 memory care units – it was not possible to operate it as an owner-operated community; therefore, we chose a very well respected third-party operator, Life Care Services.

When we had the opportunity to acquire, in partnership with a third-party real estate investment partnership, three existing senior living communities, bringing onboard some 420 additional units, we again chose Life Care Services as our third-party operator.

However, as time has gone on, and as we have had an opportunity to experience the pluses and minuses of each of the business models, a fourth model has been emerging. At this point, not having any particular name in the industry, I simply call it a Collaborative Management Model. Let me use an analogy to introduce the concept.

As you might recall from your history books, at its height, the Roman empire stretched from modern day Scotland in the north, throughout Europe and into the area now occupied by Iraq.

It goes without saying that Rome was in the empire building business, not unlike some of the super-sized senior living conglomerates. However, conquering is one thing; governing is a whole lot different. Given the proper resources, anyone can conquer. But not everyone can lead, or manage.

Once conquered the Romans installed a governor to govern in that area or province. Perhaps the most famous Roman governor of all time was a man by the name of Pontius Pilate who managed a small "backwater" village known as Jerusalem.

Typically, the governor chosen came from one of two places – either from an aristocratic Roman family or a successful and "Roman friendly" aristocrat in that local region. In the parlance of today, we might call that governing through a local partner rather than sending a corporate bigwig from headquarters.

Keeping this in mind, history showed us that the best governance in the Roman empire occurred through a local partner rather than through a Roman aristocrat. The locals understand the region, demographics, and cultural norms.

The fourth model, in short, represents a collaboration between an owner and a third-party. The independent becomes both the *owner and the operator*, in collaboration with an institutional third-party which tends to have wide and deep resources to bring to the relationship. Nobody knows the community better than the owner and for that reason, it is the owner who should be operating. But, the owner also needs to have the peace of mind, as do the residents in the community, that the resources are available to service and support the community if needed. For that, a large-scale third-party is appropriate.

That collaborative model continues to be the model that Tuscan Gardens has been forging within our communities as we evolve in our growth and development. Why, you might ask? Because execution matters. And execution needs to occur at the ground level, or what I call, *The Last 10 Feet*. And it's to that concept I devote my final chapter – the "Epilogue."

HIGHLIGHTS

1. Utilization of third-party operators has been a mainstay in the senior living rental marketplace and there continues to be a strong bench of third-party operators on a national basis.

2. The senior living industry is gravitating towards regional operators, particularly those that have adequate breadth and depth while at the same time understanding regional differences.

3. Owner-Operators have a vested interest not only in performing optimally, but in executing based on the brand promise and vision of the company.

4. Collaborative models which combine the resources and expertise of large third-party operators with the passion and vision of owners are currently being developed.

5. Regardless of how large owners and operators are, all senior living is local.

6. And, at the end of the day, regardless of architecture, design, food, and protocols, the heartbeat of effective management systems is the ability to deliver at the Last 10 Feet, where it matters the most.

CHAPTER 15

EPILOGUE
THE LAST 10 FEET

So, we come to the end of our journey, which in itself can be seen as a new beginning. It's the beginning of a revolution in reinventing senior living, complete with new ways to think about, working with and programs for seniors. We've covered a lot of ground with regard to:

- **The benefits of community vs. aging in place**

- **The variations in pay models**

- **Experiential programming**

- **Technology and its place in senior living**

- **And, much much more**

We've examined the processes and infrastructure of the classic senior living situations and all those critical SOPs that are designed to keep seniors safe, comfortable, and healthy. What we haven't covered, but what may be the most important of all is what I call *"The Last 10 Feet."*

The concept of *The Last 10 Feet*, popularized by Starbucks, refers to "what happens next" – after the investment of time, funds, and energy in creating the product. Starbucks has identified the precise systems and extraordinary care exerted in the growing, selecting, harvesting, buying, transporting, roasting, preserving, and brewing the perfect cup of coffee. Yet, all of that investment – the months, money, and manpower – it's all for nothing if *The Last 10 Feet* are destroyed by a failure of execution. Shove the cup into the customer's hand with a rude, "Here!", and watch as the lid you failed to secure properly pops off. Witness the customer's wrist doused in latte. It can be easily ruined in *The Last 10 Feet*.

In a manufacturing plant, you get 90% of the way to success when you are fully automated. As long as automation is working, you are in great shape. A great infrastructure allows you to do great things – to a point. At the end of the day, however, senior living isn't like that. Because caring for our seniors is all about *The Last 10 Feet*.

The Internet is a marvelous thing. You can shop, talk, pay bills, what have you. However, the final frontier for technology is that *Last 10 Feet*. That place where the web ends and your home begins.

A great example of a sophisticated infrastructure that supports *The Last 10 Feet* is Uber in general and UberEats in particular. There is no question that Uber disrupted multiple business models in its own right. And, when Uber launched UberEats, the disruption further affected countless other industries. The reason is that it incorporated the Internet, with the platform infrastructure of its technology, in combination with its local drivers and myriad of restaurants, through delivery at a local level. We can now use a Silicon Valley technology platform to source thousands of meal options made by local restaurants and delivered to our home – *The Last 10 Feet* – by local drivers in less than forty minutes. The robust infrastructure, combined with local cooks and drivers, solved the ultimate solution – completing the value chain.

The Last 10 Feet makes all the difference in the world. You can be the best of companies when it comes to processes, comprehensive SOPs, massive breadth, and an army of employees and third party operators, but unless you really recognize that your ability to close the value chain depends upon what you deliver in those *Last 10 Feet*, then you're not going to succeed.

I'm reminded of the importance of *The Last 10 Feet* as I gaze around the lobby of our Tuscan Gardens community in Venice, Florida. It's a gorgeous building. The art is stimulating. We have all the processes and procedures in place, but I see *The Last 10 Feet* in action, when I watch my wife, Janet, chatting with a resident over lunch or stopping for afternoon tea with another group. She knows their names. She knows their histories. She knows their personalities. She knows their families. Janet exemplifies the importance of *The Last 10 Feet*.

We have a certain resident at Tuscan Gardens. We call her La Contessa. She is 99 years old and has lived an amazing life. She actually reminds me of my mother.

La Contessa is sharp as a tack. She knows who she is. She knows the life she's lived. And she knows what she wants. She won't let you get away with a thing.

Janet went to pay a quick visit to La Contessa in her private apartment. At first glance, Janet saw fine furniture, original art on the walls and real linen on the table and immediately got who this wonderful lady is and where she is coming from. As an aside, that "quick visit" lasted 45 minutes because they each had so much to share with each other.

The Culture of Radical Intimacy I seek to create in all my business endeavors occurs in *The Last 10 Feet*. At every one of my businesses, for example, Janet and I have always presented each associate with a personalized holiday card – even when our associates eventually had reached 600 people. When I say personalized, I don't mean a "To Jake, From Larry and Janet" sort of message. We knew our associates intimately and shared something meaningful in those cards, often mentioning children by name or specific life events. It mattered to us and, considering the number of associates who have stayed in touch with us over the years, *it mattered to them.*

With our first Tuscan Gardens location, Janet and I offered personal cards to residents and associates alike as well as personally selected gifts. This tradition has now been handed down to the Executive Director of each location.

The Last 10 Feet in senior living is all about leadership and the way the resident experience is honored. It's the personal intimate relationship that each and every one of our caregivers has with every single resident in that community. That's what makes all the difference in the world.

A resident (and family) can forgive you for any number of things, but to really create a life of purpose, passion & joy (which is what this book is about), we must recognize that we need to honor our seniors at *The Last 10 Feet*. That's where it matters the most.

When it comes to senior living, there's no such thing as theoretical delivery. If I want a Ferrari, it's sufficient that I get the car I want. It doesn't really matter whether the salesman was rude. When I buy the car and drive it off the lot, the value chain is completed. That's all that matters. You can forgive a lot of stuff along the way to get your toy.

Senior living, on the other hand, is an ongoing delivery of value. How the caregiver shows you that he or she cares or how the executive director touches your family members is the completion of the value chain and it happens over and over again – daily. It's not a Ferrari you sell just once.

The value chain in senior living is ultimately completed within *The Last 10 Feet*, where all of the systems, processes, procedures, and infrastructure, meet day to day, hour to hour, and minute to minute, with the residents, their loved ones, and the associates employed at the community level.

At Tuscan Gardens, we pride ourselves on our aesthetic environment, sumptuous food, and enriching programs, but at the end of the day, what matters most is how we care on an individual basis for each and every resident and their family members. To the extent that we mess that up, we have not completed the value chain.

Everything we have covered in the preceding chapters comes down to one thing – solving for *The Last 10 Feet*. That's where our value meets our residents' needs and expectations.

May this book not only inspire us to move toward a rethinking of senior living and a redefinition of what that experience can mean, but may it also lead us to elegantly deliver it where it matters the most – in those *Last 10 Feet*.

CPSIA information can be obtained
at www.ICGtesting.com
Printed in the USA
BVOW06*2242071117
499824BV00003B/14/P